James Gr

A History of Fal

Methuen Drama

Published by Methuen Drama 2009

1 3 5 7 9 10 8 6 4 2

Methuen Drama
A & C Black Publishers Limited
36 Soho Square
London W1D 3QY
www.methuendrama.com

ISBN 978 1 4081 2290 7

A CIP catalogue record for this book is available from the British Library

Typeset by Country Setting, Kingsdown, Kent CT14 8ES
Printed and bound in Great Britain by
CPI Cox and Wyman, Reading RG1 8EX

A HISTORY OF FALLING THINGS

James Graham

Cast in order of appearance

Robin	Sion Pritchard
Jacqui	Katie McGuinness
Jimmy	Francois Pandolfo
Reece	Ifan Huw Dafydd
Lesley	Di Botcher
John (Voice)	Philip Bretherton
Boy	Matthew Cavallini, Adam Walker (Mold), Tomaso Dimech, Ioan Lloyd (Cardiff)
Director	Kate Wasserberg
Designer	Mark Bailey
Lighting	Tom White
Sound	Kevin Heyes
Animator	Paddy Molloy
Choreographer	Francesca Jaynes
Stage Manager On The Book	Eleanor Randall
Assistant Stage Manager	Tracey Booth

Eating, drinking and smoking are not permitted in the auditorium, and the use of cameras and tape recorders is strictly prohibited.
Please be sure to turn off digital watches and mobile phones during the performance.

First performed at Clwyd Theatr Cymru Thursday 23 April – Saturday 9 May 2009
Dydd Iau 23 Ebrill – Dydd Sadwrn 9 Mai

Sherman Theatre, Cardiff, Tuesday 12 – Saturday 16 May 2009
Dydd Mawrth 12 – Dydd Sadwrn 16 Mai

"Some of the most consistently exciting ensemble theatre in Britain is currently being produced by Hands' Clwyd company."

★★★★★ The Guardian

Created through the vision of Clwyd County Council and its Chief Executive Haydn Rees, Theatr Clwyd was opened in 1976. Located a mile from Mold town centre the building incorporates five performance venues: the Anthony Hopkins Theatre, Emlyn Williams Theatre, Studio 2, multi-function Clwyd Room for the community, cinema and three art galleries.

Following local government reorganisation in Wales, the theatre faced closure on 1st April 1997. The new Flintshire County Council and its Leader, Tom Middlehurst, asked Terry Hands to formulate an artistic and business plan to avert this threat and take the theatre forward.

Terry Hands accepted the post of Director on 2 May 1997 and asked Tim Baker to join him as associate.

In 1998 the theatre won the Barclays/TMA Theatre of the Year award and in 1999 was designated a Welsh National Performing Arts Company by the Arts Council of Wales. The name was changed to Clwyd Theatr Cymru to reflect the theatre's new national remit and its new Welsh identity.

Subsequently the theatre has become the most productive national performing arts company in Wales.

"The nearest thing to a National Theatre of Wales..." Sunday Times

President/Llywydd Lord Kinnock
Chairman/Cadeirydd Hilary Isherwood
Director/Cyfarwyddwr Terry Hands

ASSOCIATES/AELODAU CYSWLLT

Simon Armstrong
Robert Blythe
Philip Bretherton
Alun ap Brinley
John Cording
Ifan Huw Dafydd
Manon Eames
Steven Elliott
Bradley Freegard
Sara Harris-Davies
Daniel Hawksford
Lynn Hunter
Julian Lewis Jones
Gwyn Vaughan Jones
Jenny Livsey
Steven Meo
Dyfrig Morris
Siwan Morris
Simon Nehan
Kai Owen
Vivien Parry
Christian Patterson
Robert Perkins
Victoria Pugh
Steffan Rhodri
Oliver Ryan
Owen Teale
Johnson Willis

DIRECTORS/ CYFARWYDDWYR

Tim Baker
Terry Hands
Peter Rowe

DESIGNERS/ CYNLLUNWYR

Mark Bailey
Martyn Bainbridge
Nick Beadle
Max Jones
Timothy O'Brien

COMPOSERS/ CYFANSODDWYR

Dyfan Jones
Colin Towns

DI BOTCHER

Lesley

Di was born in Port Talbot and trained at Webber Douglas.

Theatre includes: **Amazed and Surprised**, **Terrorism** and **Black Milk** (Royal Court), **A Kiss on the Bottom** (New Theatre, Cardiff and tour), **Les Misérables** (Copenhagen), **Habeas Corpus** (Northampton), **The Oyster Catchers** (Swansea), **Flesh and Blood** (Hampstead), **Sunday in the Park With George** (Leicester Haymarket), **Small Change** (Basingstoke), **Card Boys** (Bush Theatre), **Beauty and the Beast** (Dominion Theatre), **Cardiff East**, **Under Milk Wood**, **Absence of War**, **The Frogs** (National Theatre), **A Tale of Two Cities** (Soho Laundry), **Into the Woods** (Library Theatre, Manchester), **Speculators**, **A Midsummer Night's Dream** (RSC), **Trafford Tanzi** (Plymouth), **Cats** (New London Theatre).

Television and film includes: **Dustbin Baby**, **Belonging** (seven series), **Doctors**, **Katy Brand's Big Ass Show**, **Coming of Age**, **The Thick of It**, **Bleak House**, **High Hopes** (six series), **Little Britain**, **Cruise of the Gods**, **Tipping the Velvet**, **Casualty**, **'Orrible**, **People Like Us**, **Fun at the Funeral Parlour**, **Alistair McGowan Show**, **Sunburn** (BBC), **Collision** (Greenlit/BBC TV), **Albert Landers** (Onedotzero/BBC), **No Signal** (You Me 'n' Him), **Ideal**, **Tittybangbang** (three series) (Baby Cow Productions), **Murphy's Law** (BBC TV/Mespil), **Pulling** (BBC TV/Silver River), **All About George**, **Rhinoceros** (Granada), **Green Wing**, **Armando Iannucci Show** (Talkback), **Kavanagh QC** (Carlton), **Life and Debt** (HTV), **All or Nothing** (Thin Man Films), **Light in the City** (Dogo Productions), **Twin Town** (Figment Films).

This is Di's debut at Clwyd Theatr Cymru.

IFAN HUW DAFYDD

Reece

An Associate of Clwyd Theatr Cymru, Huw was born in Llanelli.

Previous work for Clwyd Theatr Cymru includes: **The Drawer Boy**, **Memory** at Clwyd Theatr Cymru, London and New York. **The Crucible**, **Silas Marner**, **Rosencrantz and Guildenstern Are Dead**, **King Lear**, **Hard Times**, **Damwain a Hap**, **Rape of the Fair Country**, **A Christmas Carol**, **Afore Night Come**, **Twelfth Night**, **Song of the Earth**, **Under Milk Wood** and **Hosts of Rebecca** - completing the Alexander Cordell Trilogy.

Other theatre work includes: Traxalla in **The Indian Queen** at the Citizens' Theatre, Glasgow; Kurt in Strindberg's **Dance of Death**, Teddy in **The Faith Healer** for Theatr Gwynedd, and **Enemy of the People** in Cardiff.

Television appearances include: **Y Glas**, **Y Palmant Aur**, **Mortimer's Law**, **Heartburn Hotel**, **Y Teulu**, **Llafur Cariad**, **The Bench**, **Foyle's War**, **In Deep Ill**, **Heart of Gold**, **Con Passionate**, **Midsomer Murders**, **Last Detective** and he plays the regular security officer John Pointer in **Holby City**.

Films: **The Silent Twins**, **The Bullion Boys**, **Gadael Lenin**, **The Proposition**, **Iâr Fach Yr Hâf**, **Coming Up Roses**, **The Life and Death of Phillip Knight**, **15**, **Cross Currents**, **Daddy's Girl**, **Abraham's Point**, **I Know You Know**, **Season of Mists**, **Martha, Jac a Sianco**, **Rise of the Gargoyles** (RHI).

Huw also filmed and directed his own documentary on the making of **Martha, Jac a Sianco.**

Radio: Bob Coves in **Station Road** (BBC

Radio Wales), Caliban in **The Tempest** and Peter Shaw in **Hole** (Radio 4).

KATIE McGUINNESS
Jacqui

Katie trained at LAMDA. Theatre credits include: **Chains of Dew** and **Tragedy of Nan** (Orange Tree Theatre), **Living Quarters** (Royal Lyceum Theatre), **Salome** (Nuffield Theatre), **An Inspector Calls** (PW Productions), **Much Ado About Nothing** (Salisbury Playhouse), **Romeo and Juliet** (Vienna English Theatre).

Film credits include: **Bombil and Beatrice** (Quest Films), **He Knew He Was Right** (Deep Indigo).

Television credits include: **Dirty Filthy Love** (Granada) and Becky in **M.I.T.** (Thames/ Talkback), **Hotel Babylon**, **Doctors** (BBC), **Seven Seconds** and **Spilt Milk**.

FRANCOIS PANDOLFO
Jimmy

Francois is from Cardiff and since graduating from East 15 Acting School in 2004 his recent work includes **Sleeping Beauty** (Newport Riverfront), **Macbeth** and **The Voyage** for Clwyd Theatr Cymru, **Bad Girls** for Polka Theatre, **The Dumb Waiter** for the Pinter Festival at the Crucible, Sheffield Theatres.

Film credits include: **SCY** for Bubblehead Productions (Stephen Parsons).

Radio credits include: **The House That Eileen Built** and **The Tinner's Corpse** for BBC Radio 4.

Television credits include: **Doctor Who** and **EastEnders**.

SION PRITCHARD
Robin

Sion trained at the Royal Welsh College of Music and Drama.

Theatre credits include: **A Midsummer Night's Dream** (Clwyd Theatr Cymru), **Blink** (FAB Theatre/Brits Off Broadway Festival, 59E59 Theatres, New York), **Bobi a Sami** (Theatr Genedlaethol Cymru), **Porth y Byddar** (Clwyd Theatr Cymru/Theatr Genedlaethol Cymru), **The Way It Was**, **The Druid's Rest**, **Hobson's Choice** (Clwyd Theatr Cymru), **Fuddy Meers** (Scamp/Arts Theatre), **Y Byd A'i Brawd** (RWCMD/Sgript Cymru), **Mr Kolpert** (Venue 13/RWCMD), **Indian Country** (Sgript Cymru), **Woyzeck** (ELAN Wales).

His film and TV credits include: **Caerdydd** (Fiction Factory), **Cowbois ac Injans** (Opus/S4C), **Talcen Caled** (Ffilmiau'r Nant/S4C), **Casualty** (BBC1), **Treflan** (Alfresco/S4C), **The Good Catch** (RWCMD/On Your Marks), **Y Golau** (Opus), **Pen Tennyn** (HTV/S4C).

Radio work includes: **Fire of the Dragon**, **Falco: The Iron Fist of Mars**, **Middlewitch** (BBC Radio), **Out of the Ordinary** (BBC Radio Wales), **My Little Eye** (Elidir).

Awards: the Spotlight Prize 2004, the James Westaway Award 2003.

PHILIP BRETHERTON
John (Voice)

Philip is an Associate of Clwyd Theatr Cymru.

Previous work here includes: **The Importance of Being Earnest**, **Blithe Spirit** and **Noises Off** directed by Terry Hands and **Present Laughter** and **An Ideal Husband** directed by Christopher Morahan.

Elsewhere, his most recent theatre work includes **Life After Scandal** at Hampstead Theatre and the Drum Theatre, Plymouth, Poliakoff's **Breaking the Silence** at Nottingham Playhouse, and **Who's Afraid of Virginia Woolf?** at the Royal Exchange Theatre, Manchester.

His television work includes **New Tricks**, **Inspector Morse**, **Miss Marple**, **Real Women**, **Heart and Bones**, **Hollyoaks** and nine years playing Alistair in **As Time Goes By** starring Judi Dench. He appeared as Duffy's husband in **Casualty** (before being killed by a psychopathic anaesthetist), as Stefan Hauser, the German Manager of Earl's Park FC in **Footballers' Wives** and as love-rat Ian Davenport in **Coronation Street**.

MATTHEW CAVALLINI
Boy

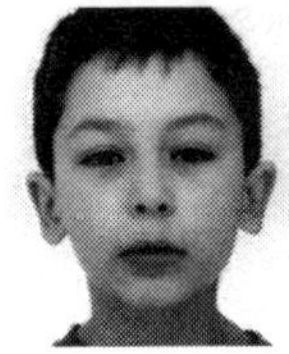

ADAM WALKER
Boy

TOMASO DIMECH
Boy

IOAN LLOYD
Boy

JAMES GRAHAM
Writer

26-year-old James was the winner of the inaugural Catherine Johnson Best Play award in 2007 (for **Eden's Empire**), and was named a 2008 television hotshot by *Broadcast* magazine. He was part of the BBC and Royal Court's 'The 50' writers' initiative to mark the theatre's anniversary in 2006. James is writer-in-residence at the Finborough Theatre in London where his plays have included **Albert's Boy**, starring Victor Spinetti as Albert Einstein (recipient of a Pearson Playwriting Bursary); **Eden's Empire**; and **Little Madam**, based on the childhood of Margaret Thatcher. Last summer, James had two Time Out Critics' Choice shows playing simultaneously in London – **Tory Boyz** at the Soho Theatre and **Sons of York** at the Finborough. He is currently under commission at the Bush and the National Youth Theatre, and his stage adaptation of **The Adventures of Huckleberry Finn** for Shapeshifter and Fresh Glory will be touring in spring 2010.

For the screen, James's original comedy-drama **Caught in a Trap** was ITV1's Boxing Day drama last Christmas. He is currently developing and writing drama series with Carnival Films and World Productions for the BBC.

His first radio play **How You Feeling, Alf?** will be broadcast on BBC Radio 4 this spring.

KATE WASSERBERG
Director

Kate has recently joined Clwyd Theatr Cymru as New Plays Director. Previous to this she was Associate Director of the Finborough Theatre, London, where she directed **Sons of York** and **Little Madam**, both by James Graham and **The Representative**, **I Wish to Die Singing** and **The New Morality**. Other directing includes 2007 Schools Festival (Young Vic), **Switzerland** (Hightide Festival), **Doing Lines** (Pleasance), **Blue Velvet** (Gilded Balloon), **The Studio** (South West tour) and **The Firebird** (Exeter Phoenix).

As an Assistant Director Kate has worked at the Barbican, the Abbey Theatre Dublin, the Young Vic, Shakespeare's Globe and the Theatre Royal Bath.

MARK BAILEY
Designer

Mark Bailey has designed over one hundred productions in Britain, Europe and North America.

He is an Associate Artist of Clwyd Theatr Cymru where his many designs include: **Noises Off**, **Great Expectations**, **The Suicide**, **A Midsummer Night's Dream**, **An Ideal Husband**, **Of Mice and Men**, **The Way It Was**, **Present Laughter**, **A Chorus of Disapproval**, **The Druid's Rest**, **Hobson's Choice**, **Brassed Off**, **Hay Fever**, **Waiting for Godot**, **One Flew Over the Cuckoo's Nest**, **Pleasure and Repentance**, **Accidental Death of an Anarchist**, **Hard Times**, **Portrait of the Artist as a Young Dog**, **Oleanna**, **A View From the Bridge**, **Blithe Spirit**, **Oh What a Lovely War**, **To Kill a Mockingbird**, **The Four Seasons**, **Silas Marner**, **Betrayal**, **The Rabbit**, **King Lear**, **Private Lives** and the Alexander Cordell Trilogy (**Rape of the Fair Country**, **Hosts of Rebecca** and **Song of the Earth**).

Recent designs include: **Macbeth** for the Chicago Shakespeare Theatre, **Privates on Parade** at West Yorkshire Playhouse, and in the West End **Legal Fictions** starring Edward Fox (Savoy) and **Rent** at the Duke of York's, **The Snow Queen** for English National Ballet and set for **The Rise and Fall of the City of Mahagonny** for Los Angeles Opera. Other work includes **Hamlet** (Chicago Shakespeare Theatre), national tours of **The Rivals** and **Mack and Mabel** (also in the West End); **To Reach the Clouds** (Nottingham Playhouse), **The Importance of Being Earnest** (Oxford Playhouse); **The Threepenny Opera** (National Theatre and tour); **Rat Pack Confidential** (West End/Nottingham Playhouse); **The Resistible Rise of Arturo Ui** (Glasgow Citz).

Designs for music and dance include **Melody on the Move** (English National Ballet), **Iolanthe** (Savoy), **Ariadne auf Naxos** (Maggio Musicale Florence and Opera de Lausanne), **Il Maestro di Capella**, **Susanna's Secret** and **The Telephone** (Buxton Festival), **Carmen** (ROH Linbury Studio), **Ladders and Snakes** (Opera North), and **False Love/True Love** and **What Price Confidence?** (Almeida Opera). He has also designed **Into the Woods** (Theatre Royal,York), **Cabaret**, **Irma La Douce**, **Fiddler on the Roof** and **The Gondoliers** (also West End) all for the Watermill, Newbury, all of which won or were nominated for TMA Best Musical awards.

Other work in London includes national tours of **Entertaining Mr Sloane** (Greenwich); **Peace in Our Time**, **A Chorus of Disapproval** and **Hadrian VII** (Richmond) and **The Importance of Being Earnest** (Old Vic/Toronto); **The Winslow Boy** (Gielgud), **A Judgement in Stone** (Lyric Hammersmith), costumes for **Which Which** (Piccadilly) and **Present Laughter** (Aldwych and Wyndham's).

Mark has also designed **Broken Lives** for BBC Television.

TOM WHITE
Lighting Designer

Tom trained at Middlesex University and graduated from the Technical Theatre Arts course in 2004. Tom now lights a variety of productions ranging from medium-scale UK tours to international musicals and operettas. His work has been seen in Egypt, Italy, Romania, Austria, Spain and France. He works regularly with Tangled Feet (Stage award and Fringe First nominees 2007/8), BRAWL a company based in the UK and Proyecto Opera based in Valladollid Spain.

Tom's other production role credits include the **BBC Electric Proms**, the **Paris Autoshow 2008**, **Longborough Festival Opera**, **Whipping It Up** (West End and UK tour), the Roundhouse, the Wrestling School Company, the Bush Theatre and Paines Plough.

Recent theatre credits: **Where's My Desi Soulmate** (Theatre Royal Stratford East and tour), **Sons of York** (Finborough Theatre), **The Halo Project** (Bush Theatre), **50 Ways to Leave Your Lover** (Bush Theatre),**The Pink Bedroom** (Courtyard Theatre), **Weapons of Happiness** (Finborough Theatre), **Little Madam** (Finborough Theatre), **Poofloose with Stephen De Martin**, **1 Poof and a Piano** (Udderbelly), **Game?** by Tangled Feet (Theatre 503 then UK tour), **Hedda Gabler** (Teatrul Bulandra in Bucharest, Romania), **Love Child** (Finborough Theatre), **Mozart's Back** (Assembly Rooms), **Emily's Kitchen** (Gilded Balloon), **The Representative** (Finborough Theatre), **Hamlet and Malvolio and His Masters** (Southwark Playhouse), **Deir Yassan Day** (Bloomsbury Theatre), **Yesterday Was a Weird Day** (BAC), **Cargo** (Northern School of Contemporary Dance), **Catching Dust** by Tangled Feet (Teatro Della Contraddizione, Milan, Italy), **Miss Julie** (Greenwich Playhouse), **Snapshots** and **Maybe Baby** (Old Red Lion Theatre), **A Servant of Two Masters** (New End Theatre Hampstead), **Sotoba Komachi** and **The Damask Drum** (Greenwich Playhouse).

Opera credits include:**The Marriage of Figaro** (UK tour), **Simon Boccanegra** (Feria De Valladollid, Spain), **The Immortal Orchestra in Concert** (The Roundhouse in Camden), **The Crocodile** (Arcola Theatre as part of the 'Grimeborn season').

Musical credits: **Sleeping Beauty** (Broadway Theatre, Barking), **Alyona** (Theatre am Lend, Graz, Austria), Shola Ama and special guests in concert (Roundhouse).

KEVIN HEYES
Sound Designer

Came to Clwyd Theatr Cymru in 1984 from Leeds Playhouse to join the lighting and sound department. He has been designing lighting and sound for shows ever since, in the Anthony Hopkins Theatre and the Emlyn Williams Theatre, as well as theatres throughout Wales and in Europe. He also teaches lighting and sound design at Scarborough University College and in various colleges around Wales. He redesigned the sound systems in the Anthony Hopkins Theatre and the Emlyn Williams Theatre, with the latest state-of-the-art sound equipment using full digital systems. A big part of his life is now designing firework displays all over Wales and the North West.

Some of his lighting designs include **The Way It Was**, **Flora's War**, **The Secret**, **The Ballad of Megan Morgan**, **Mrs Warren's Profession**, **Our Country's Good**, **The Daughter-in-Law**, **Silas Marner**, **Misalliance** and **My Sister in This House**.

He has now turned his attention full time to sound and all that goes with it. Credits include: **Godspell**, **Gulliver's Travels**, **Swallows and Amazons**, **The Snow Queen**, **Rape of the Fair Country**, **A Christmas Carol**, **The Norman Conquests** trilogy, **Aladdin**, **Flora's War**, **Song of the Earth**, **Dick Whittington**, **Hard Times**, **Cinderella - The Panto With Soul**, **King Lear**, **Bedroom Farce**, **The Rabbit**, **Jack**

and the Beanstalk, Rosencrantz and Guildenstern Are Dead, The Four Seasons, Robin Hood and the Babes in the Wood, Oh What a Lovely War, The Ballad of Megan Morgan, Aladdin - the Red Hot Wok 'n' Roll Panto, One Flew Over the Cuckoo's Nest, Hay Fever, The Mabinogion, Brassed Off, Sleeping Beauty - The Rock 'n' Roll Panto, Troilus and Cressida, A Streetcar Named Desire, Sugar, The Way It Was, Dick Whittington - The Rock 'n' Roll Panto, Present Laughter, An Inspector Calls, Beauty and the Beast, Of Mice and Men, Suddenly Last Summer, A Toy Epic, Jack and the Beanstalk, Cariad, The Suicide, Cinderella - The Panto With Soul and **Great Expectations**.

PADDY MOLLOY

Animator

Paddy Molloy trained in Illustration and Animation at Kingston University, graduating in 2004. He recently produced animated projections and artwork for Theatre O and Enda Walsh's **Delirium** (West Yorkshire Playhouse, Abbey Theatre, Barbican 2008) and as an illustrator, Paddy regularly contributes to *The Guardian* (UK) and the *Globe* and *Mail* (Canada) as well as producing bespoke work for clients including *The New York Times*, *Time Out*, *Big Issue* and Random House.

Paddy lives and works in London.

FRANCESCA JAYNES

Choreographer

For Clwyd Theatr Cymru: **Cinderella, Beauty and the Beast, Leader of the Pack, Sugar, Happy End, Rape of the Fair Country, Hosts of Rebecca, Sweeney Todd, Silas Marner, Aladdin** and **The Cavalcaders**.

Other theatre work includes: **After Life, The Threepenny Opera** and **The Day After Tomorrow** for the National Theatre; **My Best Friend** for Hampstead Theatre; **On the Piste, The Entertainer, Pinocchio, Toad of Toad Hall** and **Romeo and Juliet** for Birmingham Rep; **Blues in the Night, Little Shop of Horrors** and **A Funny Thing Happened on the Way to the Forum** for the New Wolsey, Ipswich; and work for the Liverpool Everyman, Chester Gateway, Belgrade Coventry, Theatre Royal York and the London Bubble.

Films include: **The Duchess, Sweeney Todd, Prince of Persia, Me and Orson Welles, The Picture of Dorian Gray, The Da Vinci Code, Charlie and the Chocolate Factory, Vera Drake, De-Lovely, A.I. Artificial Intelligence** and **Topsy-Turvy** (American choreography Awards nomination).

Work in television includes **Elizabeth the Virgin Queen, Hustle, Miss Marple, Foyle's War, Byron, Tipping the Velvet, Sons and Lovers, The Vice, In a Land of Plenty** and **A Life for a Life Stefan Kiszko**.

CLWYD THEATR CYMRU

CLWYD THEATR CYMRU BOARD OF GOVERNORS

Fiona Allan
Cllr Chris Bithell
David Brierley
Cllr Ron Davies
Robert Ellis
Keith Evans
Colin Everett
Cllr Robin Guest
Cllr George Hardcastle
Cllr Patrick Heesom
Cllr Mel Higham
Cllr Hilary Isherwood
Cllr Peter Macfarlane
Cllr Nancy Matthews
Prof Michael Scott
Geraint Stanley Jones
Sandra Wynne
Cllr Helen Yale

PRESIDENT [illegible] | **CHAIRMAN** Cllr Hilary Isherwood | **DIRECTOR** Terry Hands

ASSOCIATE DIRECTOR
Tim Baker

GENERAL MANAGER
Julia Grime

ASSOCIATE DIRECTOR: PLAYS & TOURING
William James

DIRECTOR: NEW PLAYS
Kate Wasserberg

CASTING
Leigh-Ann Regan

PA TO THE DIRECTORS
Melanie Jones

ASSISTANT TO GENERAL MANAGER
Craig Williams

EDUCATION

EDUCATION PRODUCER
Anne Plenderleith

EDUCATION ADMINISTRATOR
Nerys Edwards

EDUCATION CO-ORDINATOR
Jane Meakin

DRAMA OUTREACH WORKER
Emyr John

TUTORS
Carolyn Davies-Moore, Clare-Louise Edwards, Claire Howard, Zoë Knapman, Jenny Stockbridge, Laura Welsby

FINANCE

FINANCIAL MANAGER
Emma Sullivan

FINANCE ASSISTANTS
Sandra Almeida, Carol Parsonage

GALLERIES

GALLERY CURATOR
Jonathan Le Vay

MARKETING

MARKETING MANAGER
Ann Williams

SPONSORSHIP MANAGER
Annie Dayson

BOX OFFICE MANAGER
Marie Thorpe

PRESS OFFICER
Anthony Timothy

DEPUTY MARKETING MANAGER
Morwenna Honan

MARKETING ASSISTANT
Angharad Madog

DISTRIBUTION
Brian Swarbrick

BOX OFFICE ASSISTANTS
Carol Edwards, Rosemary Hughes, Nikki Jones, Jan Lewis, Fiona Powell, Jean Proctor, Mair Eluned Rush, Jennifer Walters, Mary Williams

PRODUCTION

PRODUCTION MANAGER
Jim Davis

DEPUTY PRODUCTION MANAGER
Hannah Lobb

TECHNICAL & DEVELOPMENT MANAGER
Pat Nelder

TECHNICAL STAGE MANAGER
Jayson Noble

DEPUTY TECHNICAL STAGE MANAGER
Paul Adams

ASSISTANT TECHNICAL STAGE MANAGERS
Angel Hasted, Scott Howard, Nic Samuel

HEAD OF WARDROBE
Deborah Knight

WARDROBE CUTTERS
Emma Aldridge, Michal Shyne

WARDROBE ASSISTANT
Alison Hartnell

COSTUME MAINTENANCE
Cath Jones, Amber Smit

HEAD OF LX & SOUND
Keith Hemming

DEPUTY HEAD LX & SOUND
Kevin Heyes

DEPUTY (LIGHTING)
Geoff Farmer

ASSISTANT ELECTRICIANS
Dan Armishaw, Gareth Hughes, Matthew Williams, Neil Williams

PROPERTIES
Eugenie Hardstone

PROPERTIES CARPENTER
Bob Heaton

HEAD OF WORKSHOP
John Wynne-Eyton

CONSTRUCTION
Steve Eccleson
Tom Parsons,
Andy Sutters

SCENIC ARTIST
Mike Jones

WIG MISTRESS
Louise Penman

THEATRE MANAGEMENT

THEATRE MANAGER
Kenneth Anthonisz

BUILDING SERVICES MANAGER
Jim Scarratt

HOUSE MANAGER
Marion Wright

ASSISTANT FRONT OF HOUSE MANAGERS
Maivena Bingham, Elena Vedovotto

SHOP MANAGER
Wendy Dawson

RECEPTIONISTS/BOOKSHOP
Carole Adams (Relief), Emma Brunt, Elaine Godwin, Carole Jones, Nerys Jones, Jennifer Walters (Relief)

CLEANING SUPERVISOR
Mark Sandham

CLEANERS
Tracey D'Amato, Lorraine Jones, Maxine Kalewski, Tara Pritchard, Ann Shaw, Patricia Williams, Richard Williams

SALES ASSISTANTS
Liz Gamble, Elaine Jones, Luisa Sciarillo, Emily Thelwell, Christine Wright

BAR MANAGER
Salv Vena

RESTAURANT MANAGER
Rhian Walls

DEPUTY RESTAURANT MANAGER
Nicola Wyatt

PROJECTIONISTS
Mike Roberts
Mike Batchellor (Relief)
Matthew Wright (Relief)

STAGE MANAGEMENT

COMPANY STAGE MANAGER
Helen Drew

STAGE MANAGERS (on the book)
Eleanor Randall, Edward Salt

STAGE MANAGER
Kelly Hodder

ASSISTANT STAGE MANAGERS
Tracey Booth, Nicola Ireland

ADDITIONAL STAFF FOR A HISTORY OF FALLING THINGS

DRESSER
Lindy Davies

SCENIC ARTIST
Katy Salt

CHAPERONE
Elaine Mittell

PRODUCTION PHOTOGRAPHY
Catherine Ashmore

ADDITIONAL STAFF ON TOUR

WARDROBE SUPERVISOR
Lindy Davies

CYNGOR Sir y Fflint Flintshire COUNTY COUNCIL

CYNGOR CELFYDDYDAU CYMRU / THE ARTS COUNCIL OF WALES

Noddir gan Lywodraeth Cynulliad Cymru / Sponsored by Welsh Assembly Government

A History of Falling Things

Characters

Robin
Jacqui

Lesley, *Robin's mum*
Reece, *Jacqui's dad*
Jimmy, *a courier*
Boy

John, *Robin's psychologist (voice only)*

A Note on the Text

A forward slash (/) indicates that the next speaker overlaps at this point.

(Speech in brackets) indicates that the line is spoken internally/ sotto voce.

> Speech that is indented thus indicates that a character is addressing the audience directly.

A **Boy** *stands, waiting. He wears kneepads, a cycling helmet, and a rucksack.*

A shoe falls from the sky and hits the **Boy** *on his head. The* **Boy** *looks around and sees the shoe on the floor. He picks it up. He looks up at the sky, then back at the shoe. He looks up at the sky, then back at the shoe. He looks up at the sky . . .*

He puts the shoe in his bag and leaves . . .

A kitchen table. The **Boy** *goes and sits under it, replacing his cycling helmet with a saucepan. From his rucksack he retrieves some books.*

The **Boy** *looks out from under the table, up towards the sky. He takes out a Walkman and puts on a pair of headphones, pressing play.*

Music.

The **Boy** *opens a book and begins to read, all the time taking intervals to look out from the table, up toward the sky.*

Fade to black, as the music grows . . .

Lights up on the kitchen table. **Robin** *is sitting underneath it, scribbling in a notebook. A laptop nearby. As the music fades, he looks up to the sky, then carries on writing. He looks over what he's done.*

Robin (*reading*) ' "Will you play . . . " '

Scribbles something out. Rewrites.

' "Can I play with you?" Pluto said.
As Mars and Venus shook their head.
"But why not?" Pluto did say' –

No, that's crap. (Say, may, way . . . play?) Play?

(*Writing.*) 'Pluto was . . .

'Pluto was sad. "Why can't I play?"
You let me join in yesterday." ' (Yes.)
"You aren't one of us," hissed Saturn
As the rest began their circling pattern,
And no matter how much Pluto tried,
He just had to watch. Alone. Outsi– '

A beep from the computer. **Robin** *leans over and checks it.*

Robin Oh. Hello. Where did you come from?

Blackout.

The voices of **Robin** *and* **John**, *talking over the phone.*

John (*off*) Where are you now?

Robin (*off*) What do you mean?

John (*off*) You know what I mean, Robin. Where are you speaking to me from? Are you under the table again?

Robin (*off*) I . . . (*Sighs.*) I'm moving around. I'm –

John (*off*) All right. All right. So, what's new? How are you doing?

Robin (*off*) Nothing's . . . I've – there's – I'm never any different. John. Nothing changes. Since yesterday, since the day before, since . . . well, since then, really.

John (*off*) But now you're a man.

Robin (*off*) But hardly anything has changed. / That's my –

John (*off*) And whose fault is that?

Robin (*off*) What?

John (*off*) And whose fault is that, Robin?

Robin (*off*) I'm not finding this particularly helpful today.

John (*off*) Because you aren't trying. And you're not paying for it, she is.

Robin (*off*) Pay . . . (*Sighs.*) Paying for me to get worse. / (Waste of money.)

John (*off*) You aren't getting worse. What was that?

Robin (*off*) I'm . . . I'm staying – it – that, that's what I'm – it, it, it –

John (*off*) Calm down, take a breath.

Robin (*off*) It – I wasn't –

John (*off*) Calm down.

Robin (*off*) I wasn't stuttering, I was, I was emphasising. Just –

John (*off*) Just calm down.

Robin (*off*) I'm staying the same, is what I'm saying. So this, this can't be helping –

John (*off*) You're not getting worse, though, are you? Maybe if we didn't speak, if we didn't have these little chats, you *would* be getting worse. Ipso facto, you're getting better.

Robin (*off*) (Ipso facto.)

John (*off*) One minute, Robin, and then I have to go.

Robin (*off*) I need to tell you something.

John (*off*) What?

Robin (*off*) Before you hang up. Um. (Urgh.) OK.

John (*off*) Go on.

Robin (*off*) I'd like *her* to hear about it, but not – I don't want her to hear about it in a way that makes it sound like I've said it to you so that you'll say it to her, because even though I *am*, that will make it sound bigger than it is, when it –

John (*off*) Robin, please.

Robin (*off*) I've met someone.

John (*off*) You've met someone?

Robin (*off*) I've. Met someone.

John (*off*) You. You've Met Someone, I don't under– How? Are we talking about a girl? How?

Robin (*off*) Just . . . feeling around. In the dark. Trying to find something. My world, it's so . . . and in the middle of the darkness. After lots – after scrabbling around. I found her.

John (*off*) Sorry, wait, she's . . . how did you find her?

Robin (*off*) I just, (*Laughing.*) I just typed it in.

John (*off*) Typed it in?

Robin (*off*) Into one of the things, the search engines, just typed it in.

On a screen, a flashing curser types out the word as he spells it.

Robin (*off*) K-E-R-A-U-N-O-T-H-N-E-T-O-P-H-O-B-I-A. Keraunothnetophobia.

'A fear of falling satellites'.

The screen disappears. Darkness again.

Just like that. And there's this chat – this chatroom type thing and everyone – from all over the world, everyone just . . . some nutters at first. But then. This *girl.* Right here, who lives right . . . and so I just . . . I just typed –

He can be heard onstage, which is still in darkness. Typing.

Robin Hello.

Robin (*off – back on the phone*) And so she typed –

Jacqui *can be heard on stage, still in darkness. Typing.*

Jacqui Hello.

Robin Hello. (*Laughing.*) Hi.

Jacqui Hi. How are you?

Robin I'm OK. Thank you. How are you?

Jacqui I'm OK. Would you like to see me?

Robin What do you . . . how do / you mean?

Jacqui See each other, I mean, sorry. Do you have a webcam?

Robin (*off, on the phone*) And so, bing. Light.

Jacqui *appears in a spot, stage left.* **Robin** *can still only be heard.*

Jacqui Hello?

Robin Hello. Wow (sorry.) I (shit) I –

Jacqui Can you see me? You're not on.

Robin What?

Jacqui I can't see you.

Robin Oh. I can see you.

Jacqui Something's wrong. Is it installed?

Robin Let me . . . (piece of) . . . sorry. One second.

Jacqui (*waiting*) Feels weird, being looked at when . . . when I can't see –

Robin There.

Robin *appears in a light, stage right. They look at each other.*

Robin How's that?

Jacqui Oh. Yes. There you are. (*Beat. Smiles.*) Hello.

Robin Hello. (*Laughing.*) Sorry. I've . . . I've never done this before.

Jacqui Oh God, no. No, me neither. Not really.

Robin So, is your name really CityKitten84 or . . . ?

Jacqui Huh. Um. It's Jacqui.

Robin Robin. Hello.

Jacqui Hi. (*Pause.*) You're how I imagined actually.

Robin Really?

Jacqui From what you've – the things you written to . . . in the chatroom. Thing. Yeah. A bit. (*Giggles.*) I'm embarrassed, sorry.

Robin You look . . .

Jacqui What?

Robin (*pause*) Really . . .

Jacqui (*beat; giggles*) What?

Robin (*beat; shrugs*) Perfect.

> **Jacqui** (*speaking out*) He didn't say that.
>
> **Robin** Yes I did.
>
> **Jacqui** No.
>
> **Robin** In my *head* that's what I said.
>
> **Jacqui** But out of your mouth came . . . ?
>
> **Robin** It had been a while. I was out of practice.
>
> **Jacqui** He said I looked 'good'. 'In the face.'
>
> **Robin** That *is* what I said. But you found it funny.
>
> **Jacqui** I found it charming. In a bumbling kind of way. (*Laughing.*) 'You look good in the face.'
>
> **Robin** Thank you.
>
> **Jacqui** No. Thank you.

Jacqui So that's your place. Let me see.

As **Robin** *turns and looks around, light spreads across his living room, stage right.*

What we see is half a room, cut off in the middle. At the cut-off point, the furniture there too is cut in half. Half a bookcase, half a sofa, a door at the rear, a desk at the back, etc. It's evening . . .

Robin Just your average living room in your average house / in your –

Jacqui Detached, semi-detached, flat?

Robin House. Terraced.

Jacqui Ha! Mine too. Is it yours?

Robin Yes. What do you mean?

Jacqui Do you own it?

Robin Oh no. No, God, no way. I rent it.

Jacqui Right. Course.

Robin But I rent it On My Own. That's what I thought you –

Jacqui Yeah, no. It's very nice.

Robin Even round here, now, prices have . . . even now, it –

Jacqui Lots of books.

Robin Yeah, lots of books. I – that's what I – I'm a writer.

Jacqui A writer? Really?

Robin That's how I . . . you know, survive.

Jacqui What do you write?

Robin You know. Books. Things. Children's books.

Jacqui Ha! That's really cool.

Robin Well. And yours? You, yours?

Jacqui Oh. Just . . .

She turns and looks around, as light spreads round her bedroom, also cut in half, so that, apart from the difference in appearance, they could perhaps be two halves of the same room, with a 'no man's land' of darkness centre stage, between them.

Jacqui*'s bedroom looks like that of a young girl. Single bed. Bright colours . . .*

Robin Wow. God, so that's your –

Jacqui I know what you're thinking.

Robin I'm not / thinking anything.

Jacqui It's my old room. I've had it since I was, like, six. So . . .

Robin Was it weird. Coming back?

Jacqui It was depressing. And yet a little bit . . . I don't know. A little bit not.

Robin Different from London.

Jacqui Uh, yeah. Ahuh. Yeah, different from London.

Robin But 'home', though.

Jacqui Yeah. Nice to have my dad close again. In some ways.

Robin How close?

Jacqui His bedroom is next door.

Robin That must be weird.

Jacqui Yeah, a little. Everyone is trying hard to understand. It's not easy for them. Particularly Dad.

Robin It's not easy for anyone.

Jacqui He says I've lost my accent.

Robin Yeah, my folks said that. When I came back from uni. You get it back, though.

Jacqui You went to uni?

Robin Yeah. Well, kinda. For a bit.

Jacqui It just sounded like . . . from the things you posted on the . . . on the thing. It just sounded like you'd been like this. For a while.

Robin I didn't finish. It got too . . . um, 'much'. But I've done – I did one of those, uh, Open University thingies instead. From here. From home.

Jacqui Oh, right. OK. Well done.

Robin I'm glad you moved back. It's nice to feel like someone is close. For what it's worth.

Jacqui Yeah. Well. For what it's worth.

Robin Right. What?

Jacqui Well, you may as well be in Dubai or, or, you know –

Robin Sure.

Jacqui But no, you're right, it's nice. For what it's worth. (*Beat. Referencing her clothes.*) I wish I'd put something nicer on. This –

Robin Don't be – you look so. Nice.

Jacqui Well. Thank you. I . . . (*Looks down at herself.*)

> **Jacqui** (*speaking out*) I knew what he was thinking.
>
> **Robin** I wasn't.
>
> **Jacqui** You were. You thought I'd planned it, got done up to look good for you.
>
> **Robin** Well I, it had crossed my mind. / But I liked that.
>
> **Jacqui** Well, I didn't. When I'm working, even now it's from home, if I am working, it helps, it helps me to feel smart. Like I'm out there. It wasn't for you.
>
> **Robin** OK, OK.

Robin *disappears.* **Jacqui** *faces out and mouths 'It was' to us.* **Robin** *reappears.*

Jacqui So I'll see you again? Maybe tomorrow?

Robin Yeah. Tomorrow's good.

Blackout.

Robin *and* **John** *over the phone again.*

John (*off*) Have the dreams changed since you met? What fell in your dream last night?

Robin (*off*) Rain, at first. Like always. And then frogs.

John (*off*) Oh the frogs are back, are they? I thought we'd got rid of the frogs.

Robin (*off*) No. They're back. And then it was pennies.

John (*off*) Pennies from heaven, ey? And then the usual.

Robin (*off*) There was something else. Before the usual.

John (*off*) Before the satellite? What?

Robin (*off*) . . . Blood.

John (*off*) Blood?

Robin (*off*) Yes.

John (*off*) That's a new one.

Robin (*off*) What do you think it means?

John (*pause, off*) Probably nothing.

Robin *and* **Jacqui** *on their respective sides.*

Jacqui What started you writing for children?

Robin I just. (*Shrugs.*) Wanted to tell stories. Loved them growing up. Even though they generally scared the shit out of me. Think children's stories can be the scariest of all. *Watership Down*, do you remember that? Rabbits being eaten by dogs or shot or run over by cars; that was nice.

Jacqui I was big into Disney. Used to dress up, had a little crown and everything. My mum bought me this music box. Spinning princess in it. Still have it. (Loser.) She used to sing this song to me and then she found this box, in a shop somewhere, that was playing the same thing. And she couldn't believe it. So she bought it for me to have when she wasn't here.

Which was more and more, as it goes.

Robin (*beat*) *Chicken Licken*, course. The chicken who believed the sky was falling down.

Jacqui Yeah, course. Even though it wasn't.

Robin Even though it wasn't. Robin Hood.

Jacqui Your namesake.

Robin Exactly. Used to pretend. Save Maid Marian. From the castle.

Jacqui There aren't any Jacquis in fairytales. Sucks. No one cool was ever called Jacqui.

Robin Jackie Kennedy.

Jacqui Oh yeah. S'pose.

Robin *The Snowman*. See, that was scary.

Jacqui That wasn't scary.

Robin Uh, the Snowman melts to death at the end.

Jacqui Oh yeah.

Robin I'm telling you. Kids' stories.

Jacqui Well, I guess it's about helping them learn.

Robin Learn what?

Jacqui That life is full of danger. And sadness. And disappointment.

Robin Well, they certainly gave me nightmares.

Jacqui I get nightmares. My whole . . . my thing started with . . . you know . . .

Robin Did it?

Jacqui It's getting late again. I should probably –

Robin Yeah. Course.

Jacqui (*beat*) Sweet dreams.

Jacqui *disappears. The middle area between the two rooms opens out, as* **Robin** *enters the space, holding an umbrella. It's raining. Music.*

Robin Cats and dogs. From what I can tell it has never ever rained cats and dogs anywhere. What has been recorded though is frogs . . .

It starts to rain frogs.

Lots and lots of frogs. Above Minneapolis in 1901, a green cloud appeared overhead, and a deluge began. While driving through Scotland in 1955, falling frogs pelted Nellie Straw's car. They fell again as recently as 1981 in Nephalion, Greece, where frogs, at the time, were not even indigenous. They are now. The only hypothesis the scientists can cling to is the waterspout phenomenon, where animals are sucked up into the sky and carried through clouds before being dropped over land. Then there's the fish.

It starts to rain fish.

Some perch fish showered a parking lot in Northern Australia, some four hundred miles from the sea. Catfish, bream and bass rained down over Alabama in 1956. Local legend records that they were very, very tasty.

It starts to rain notes, and then coins.

Lucky were a French community in 1957 when thousand-franc notes floated down over their village from a clear blue sky. Less lucky, depending on how you look at it, were the party of schoolchildren being walked home in Manchester, 1982, when they began to be pelted with pennies. The more resourceful ones not injured gathered as much as they could and ran straight to the nearest sweet shop. Stranger still, the coins that fell over Gorky in Russia were from the sixteenth century and could not be accounted for.

Various objects now begin to rain down.

The house in Evans, Colorado, that for the past one hundred and twenty odd years has suffered the occasional shower of corn, battering its roof. Then there is the as yet unproven myth of the Japanese fishing boat sunk off the coast of Siberia – the traumatised crew insisting wholeheartedly that the hole in the middle of the deck was caused by nothing other than . . . a cow. Falling from above.

It begins to rain blood.

And in Li Yan, France, and in Calabria, Italy, and in California, and in India, where recorded, falling from the sky, were tiny little droplets of scarlet red blood . . .

Electronic beeps. **Robin** *looks up as a shadow is cast over him. The sound of a heavy object plummeting to the ground.* **Robin** *ducks. The noise is cut off instantly by:*

Jacqui *and* **Robin** *on their respective sides. Drinking tea.*

Robin You've never seen it.

Jacqui Is it that one with the aliens?

Robin No, that's *Close Encounter. Brief Encounter* is the black-and-white one. With the train station? We could watch it together. Well, not together, but . . . you know. At the same time.

Jacqui Yeah, OK. Like a date.

Robin Uh. Yeah. I . . . Do, do British people, do they go on dates? I always thought that was American.

Jacqui I went on dates. In London. Kind of.

Robin Did you?

Jacqui I like the way that women used to be kissed in the old films. The way they'd get flung around. By Clark Gable or someone, and they'd . . . (*Trying to demonstrate.*) sort of, they'd get the girl's, this hair, kind of get flicked round and lean on his hands . . .

Robin I used to love how men held guns. Be like this. (*Demonstrates.*) Elbows pointing straight out from the hip. Like that. Keeping it close. Now in films it's up and out.

Stands and holds his arm out, parallel with his shoulder, finger pointed.

Like, and legs spread apart. More showy, I suppose.

Jacqui My dad says in classic love films, the colour ones are more likely to see them get together in the end and the black-and-white ones, they're more likely to end up apart.

Robin Dunno, maybe. They end up apart in *Casablanca.* And *Brief Encounter*.

Jacqui Well, that's why life should be in full colour then.

Robin Speaking of, of, um . . . stories, I've got you – I've got a surprise for you. A present. Well it's just a book. Well it, my, it's just my book. Actually.

Jacqui Yours? Oh my God.

Robin I mean, don't . . . You know, I mean I get copies free so don't . . . it's no biggie. / But.

Jacqui Oh, don't ruin it. That's really kind. Thank you. But I can just order one online.

Robin No, I've got a courier. Coming. To, to pick it up, and bring it round.

Jacqui Robin.

Robin Don't think anything of it.

Knock at **Robin***'s door.* **Robin** *opens it.* **Jimmy**, *the courier, stands there.*

Jimmy Pick up from Robin?

Robin Hi. Yes, here. Uh, address is, is on the front.

Jimmy Cheers.

A space opens out between the rooms: the doorway to **Jacqui***'s house.*

Reece *opens the door to* **Jimmy**.

Reece Oh. Hello.

Jimmy Delivery.

Reece I didn't order a pizza.

Jimmy It's not a pizza, it's a package.

Reece A package, who for?

Jimmy For Jacqui, says here.

Reece Oh. Right. She's – that's my daughter, she's upstairs.

Jimmy Sign here, please.

Reece She's always getting packages from London, you know. Bit late for work, though.

Jimmy I don't think it was work. It comes from a boy.

Reece A boy?

Jimmy Well, a young man I suppose. Charlton Street, five minutes or so.

Reece From a boy on Charlton Street? She doesn't know any boys round here, Jacqui; she doesn't know anyone any more.

Jimmy Right.

Reece Locks herself away in her room, you see.

Jimmy Right. Have a good night then, sir.

Reece Oh yes. Right-oh. Good night.

Jacqui*'s room.* **Reece** *enters.*

Jacqui Dad.

Reece Package here.

Jacqui Thank you.

Reece From a boy, he said, the fella.

Jacqui Uh, yeah. A friend. I've met. Sort of.

Reece A friend you've met sort of?

Jacqui Yes.

Reece (*at the computer*) What, on that thing?

Jacqui Yes.

Reece Oh. Oh right.

Jacqui Is he still here? The courier?

Reece He's just getting on his bike. (*Laughs.*) 'On yer bike', ey. Ha ha. Do you want me to bring your tea up or are you coming down?

Jacqui Dad, can you do me a favour? (*With a card.*) Can you ask him to deliver this?

Reece What's that now?

Jacqui Please, here's some money.

Reece Well, he's going, he's probably got another job –

Jacqui No, look, he's still outside on his radio.

Reece Oh Lord, all – (*Sighs, takes the card.*) Wait here.

Downstairs. **Reece** *with* **Jimmy** *at the doorway.*

Reece I am sorry.

Jimmy It's just I only had one more and then was clocking off, you see?

Reece I've got some money.

Jimmy It's not the money, I'm meant to be going out.

Reece Oh, anywhere nice?

Jimmy Just a curry. With the missus. Well, I say missus, we haven't really had that chat yet, but –

Reece I would really appreciate it. It seems to mean a lot to her, for some reason.

Jimmy (*counting the money*) I'm not sure this is enough, to be honest with you.

Reece (*taking out his wallet and more cash*) Oh, I see. Uh, there you go then.

Jimmy Oh. Thank you. Well, I'll see what I can do.

Reece You know, I reckon that's the problem with young people in cities, don't you? Because they can get anything they want instantly they have no sense of prudence. Or of waiting for anything. She could have just as well stuck a stamp on that and I'd have posted it and it could've been there the day after next, but oh no. Must have now.

Jimmy I know what you mean, sir, I know exactly what you mean.

> **Reece** (*speaking out*) We laugh about this little exchange in months to come.
>
> **Jimmy** We do, he's right.

Jimmy Good evening then, sir.

Reece Ay, go well, young man, go well.

Knock on **Robin***'s door.* **Robin** *answers.*

Robin Oh. Hello again. Was there a problem?

Jimmy Pick up and return. (*Handing him the card.*) Here. For you.

Robin From her?

Jimmy Yes, from her. Via him, from her.

Robin Via him?

Jimmy Her dad. Nice chap. I'll see you later.

Robin Wait. Could you – ?

Jimmy Oh no, no, that's it, I'm off home –

Robin No, just a question, I . . . it's just . . . I, I wanted to know. What she was. Like.

Jimmy Who? The girl?

Robin Yeah.

Jimmy You've never met?

Robin No.

Jimmy I didn't see her. She was upstairs. It was her dad who I dealt with, I'm afraid.

Robin Oh. OK.

Jimmy She seemed nice from downstairs, though.

Robin Really, you can tell?

Jimmy Sometimes you just get a vibe, don't you?

Robin Yeah. I suppose you do.

Jimmy *leaves.* **Robin** *closes the door. Begins opening the card. Turns to* **Jacqui***.*

Robin What's this?

Jacqui I just wanted . . . I don't know. I just wanted you to have something *there* that . . . I don't know, that used to be *here*. Some . . . (*Sighs.*) contact, or (I don't know).

Robin (*reads the front*) 'Congratulations on passing your driving test.' Awh.

Jacqui Sorry. Only one I had. For my nephew.

Robin Oh, I'm sorry, you shouldn't have –

Jacqui No that's OK, he won't pass. Least I bloody hope not.

Robin 'Thanks for the book. Love, Jacqui.' (*Pause.*) Thank you.

Jacqui No. (*With her book.*) No, thank you.

Robin (Lovely handwriting.)

Jacqui Jesus, you must be so proud. The illustrations are beautiful. Did you do them?

Robin No.

Jacqui Well. I can't wait to read it. 'Ages five and above.' Good, I'm covered.

Robin (*sniffing the card*) Your hand cream.

> **Jacqui** You didn't do that.
>
> **Robin** No, I know. I waited till later. When I was on my own. Thought you might have found it pervy.
>
> **Jacqui** And I would have done. But also sweet.

Robin 'U-I.'

Jacqui Uh?

Robin Jacqui – 'U-I' at the end. In my head it, it's always been 'I-E'. (Strange.)

Jacqui Nope, just 'U' and 'I'. Quite boring, actually. Hate it.

Robin Oh I don't know, I . . . I quite like it. That it's just. 'U' and 'I'.

They stand smiling at each other for a while. Blackout on **Jacqui** *and her house.*

Lesley *enters* **Robin**'*s house carrying bags of food and other more random objects, such as framed photos, vases and plastic flowers, cleaning products etc. She places items, retrieves others and cleans throughout, never stopping.*

Lesley Phoah, cold outside today, Gordon Bennett, cold for May, anyway. Well, compared to last year, remember the spring we had last year, absolutely boiling, wasn't it? Too hot, I thought, but then again, think of the summer, well, whatever summer we had, which wasn't much, remember? Not that it makes much difference to you in here. Still, with the windows open and everything. So maybe that's it, maybe rotten spring means we'll actually have a bloody summer, who knows? No rhyme or reason most of the time, is there, the weather? Don't suppose it was quite the same down there, was it, when you were at what's-it. Even on a little island like this, they say there's differences, don't they? Well, you only have to look at Scotland, their weather, like another country isn't it – well, I suppose it is another country, in many ways, well, in most ways really. That accent, Christ. Got you a bit of the stew we had last night, here.

Robin (*takes it*) Thank you.

Lesley Me and your brother, he was round with the kids, don't know where she was, got the impression I wasn't meant to ask, if you know what I mean, look on the kids' face though, patently obvious – is that right, patently? blatantly? – anyhow, 'apparent', it was, they'd been rowing. Hope they sort it out. Your father and I never rowed. Above and beyond what you'd expect in a marriage, course. Nowadays, why is it nowadays you make it all so complicated? I reckon it's cos you all watch too many of them soaps.

> **Robin** I don't even ask any more. What she brings round in them bags, I don't care. I'll wake up and there'll be a new family photo on my bedside table, staring at me, but I just can't ask any more. And it makes absolutely no odds to her whether I notice or not.

Lesley Had a go at the path thing today? Outside, like John said? Couple of steps? One more each day? Reckon that's a good idea, I do.

Robin It doesn't work, Mum.

Lesley You should listen to John more, he's a very talented man.

Robin He's a waste of your money, Mum.

Lesley Right, there we are, jobs done, I'll have to get back, that phone'll be ringing off the hook and they'll be wondering where I've got to. Anything you want to tell me? Any news? That you've not brought up yet? Work stuff, or . . . social? Anything?

Robin Uh, well . . . I, I do meet people, you know, Mum, I, I have. Met someone. Sort of.

Lesley A girl? (*Laughs excitedly, covers her mouth.*) Sorry. A girl?

Robin It's no big deal, Mum, don't / get worked –

Lesley Does she come round here, then?

Robin No.

Lesley No?

Robin No, she . . . we met, we've only met online.

Lesley Online?

Robin Yes.

Lesley On that thing?

Robin Yes.

Lesley (*beat*) Well that's no good, is it?

Robin It's fine.

Lesley You don't know who it could be, could be some pervert, some fat old man.

Robin I've seen her.

Lesley You've seen her?

Robin We use a webcam.

Lesley You use a webcam?

Robin Mum, you're doing it again!

Lesley No, love, that's not right, you need more than that. It's not enough.

Robin It's no big deal.

Lesley You'll see. In the end, it's not enough. You're a human, Robin, humans need physical contact. Something you are seriously malnutritioned in – is that right? Malnourished?

Robin I'm fine, Mum.

Lesley More than that, you're a man, a growing man. And you've got urges. I know.

Robin (Oh God.)

Lesley And she'll have 'em, as well. And people may say it isn't important, but it is. You've got to be compatible. Sexually, I mean. And until / you try that, there's –

Robin Oh God, aah! (*Putting his fingers in his ears.*) Ah-la-la-ah-yaaah! Mum, Christ!

Lesley We-ell. You know I'm right. I may be your mother but I'm also a woman.

Robin I'm, I'm either going to have to hit my head against the wall until I pass out or you're going to have to stop talking. Please, please.

Lesley All right. You'll find out before long. Half an hour, that stew, see you tomorrow.

She kisses him on the cheek and leaves.

Robin *in his house,* **Jacqui** *in her room, each tying a balloon.*

Jacqui (*with a marker pen*) So what am I doing . . . ?

Robin (*with his own*) You write my name. And I write yours.

Jacqui (*laughing*) This is ridiculous.

Robin I'm telling you. Read this story once, about a girl, young girl in Scotland. Wrote her name on a balloon, let it go from her back garden. Weeks later, girl with the same name, somewhere in England, standing in *her* garden, caught it as it floated down, and turned it round to read her own name. If we will it hard enough, it'll reach me, and mine yours. Humour me. 'Any way we can', remember. Where you letting it go?

Jacqui Just out the window. You?

Robin Skylight, upstairs landing. (*Shivers.*) Ugh. Normally have to duck and run under that thing, but on this occasion, I'll make a, a . . . you know. So. Ready?

They lean into the area, centre stage, and let go of the balloons. They float up.

Music, as they watch.

Fade out.

Day. **Robin** *in his house.* **Jacqui** *is in her room.*

Jacqui (*referencing his books*) Have you read them all?

Robin I've. I've read something 'within' them all. A chapter. Or whatever.

Jacqui What are they on? Mainly.

Robin Just everything. Random things. Got car manuals up there. Gardening. Walks in Nepal. Just stuff.

Jacqui Why?

Robin (*shrugs*) It's how you learn, isn't it?

Jacqui That a French one? You speak French?

Robin Uh, *oui. Un peu.*

Jacqui You ever been?

Robin No. (*Beat. Confused.*) No, of course not.

Pause.

Jacqui I couldn't do this; just take a break like this normally. I need to feel like I'm . . . I'm still doing something, contributing. Can't get used to working from home. Maybe it's cos I'm in my old room. Bit different from Canary Wharf.

What do you miss the most? About out there. What is it that drives you crazy?

Robin (*beat; shrugs*) Nothing.

Jacqui Nothing; are you mad? I miss loads. I miss everything. I miss the city. Miss the buzz. The busyness. I miss . . . friends. I miss, I even miss having . . . (*Sighs.*) enemies. People to get one over on. Miss bars, clubs. Dancing. Dancing in a club. I miss catching someone's eye. In passing. On a train, in the street. Just sharing something. Silently. With someone you don't even know. (*Pause.*) I will get better. I will.

Robin (*beat*) What were the dreams?

Jacqui Uh?

Robin You said it started with dreams. Don't have to tell me. Just . . .

Pause.

Jacqui Erm, well. Just, you know . . . just bad. Bad dreams. It didn't actually begin with . . . satellites. It was . . . other things. At first.

Robin Me too.

Jacqui Started about three, four years – what date is it? Yeah, about four years ago. A very, erm . . . well, a very specific moment. Shall we say. I was on the Tube.

Robin The Tube? Surely one of the safest places you could be. From falling things.

Jacqui Yeah. You would think. I lived in Balham, when I was in London.

Robin 'The gateway to the south.' Huh.

Jacqui Yeah. What?

Robin Oh, just . . . Peter – it's a Peter Sellers sketch.

Jacqui Right.

Robin (*as Peter Sellers*) 'Ah, Bal-ham. The Gateway to the South.'

Jacqui Right.

Robin Sorry.

Jacqui There's this plaque. In the ticket hall. About the people that died after a bomb dropped on the high street during the blitz.

Robin I've seen pictures of that. Of the crater and the bus –

Jacqui Well anyway. That's where people would gather to be safe. Underground. But a bomb landed on the street. And rubble collapsed on to the station and shops and things fell into the crater and water pipes burst and people were crushed and buried and they died and I would often think about that – not too much – but sometimes, when I would travel to work in the morning. Thinking about what it would be like.

And then there was this morning one July.

A space opens out in the area between the rooms. A Tube seat.

Jacqui *sits in it. Sounds of the Tube travelling – it suddenly grinds to a stop.*

Jacqui I'd changed at Embankment and got on to the Circle Line. Never normally get a seat, that time of the day, Circle Line. But someone got off and I was the nearest so . . . and we were heading round to Liverpool Street. And just before we got to Aldgate, the train pulled to a halt. Nothing strange about that, always stopping. Stop, start, stop, start. Only it didn't move for, like, ten minutes. And people were grumbling and sighing. And then the lights went out.

The lights flicker, and then die. A distant howling wind seems to build as though blowing down the cavernous tunnel . . .

And at first there was that titter of laughter, like 'What next?' And then more moaning. And then eventually there was just silence. And in the dark I started getting these flashes. Like flashes of being trapped. And the tunnels collapsing in. And rubble dropping down. And it felt like the oxygen was getting less and I felt like I was getting cramped and I started to begin panicking and then –

Sound of the engines starting up, as the light flickers back on and the train moves.

– we started reversing backwards. It was when we got out that we heard a bomb had gone off. Near Aldgate East. And three more around London . . .

She leaves the 'Tube' and returns to her room.

Everyone one else . . . there was this sense of, like, 'defiance'. Or . . . of just not being afraid. And a unity in 'not being afraid', but the problem was I *was* afraid. Of something completely different, which made me feel different to everyone else. And the dreams at first were of ceilings and roofs, and then of . . . planes . . . and then of . . . well, you know what. And who knows why? Maybe because everything else felt irrational. Freak occurrences. And I know satellites must seem, to normal people, must seem irrational. Maybe I just needed something that was always up there. That could come down at any point. Just to justify the way I was feeling –

Robin Nothing irrational about it. There are over two and a half thousand satellites up there, and that's just the ones that are operating, it's like a graveyard, a car park, like in February this year, when those Russian and American ones crashed into each other –

Jacqui Thanks, Robin.

Robin Oh. Sorry.

Jacqui I had to take sabbatical. Felt like a fraud. There were some people in my office who'd lost friends over there, in New York, in our office over there when . . . and I didn't, hadn't lost anyone, then *or* now, but . . . I couldn't help it. Began to work from my flat more, hated going out. My friends, who had been supportive at first, began to . . . you know, ignore me. A bit. I wasn't great to be around, end of the day.

Robin Yeah. Yeah, a lot of people found me . . . uh, irritating. When I had . . . 'people' . . .

Jacqui Eventually they, they agreed I could pretty much do most of it from here. If I wanted to move back up. Be around family. Full time. And over time I just . . . (*Shrugs.*) stopped leaving altogether . . .

But I'm gonna beat it. I am going to get better. So . . .

But I mean you, you've been . . . well. Like this. For ever.

Robin Well. In degrees. Since I was a little boy. I mean, I'd always had the need to feel . . . I dunno, enclosed, I suppose. Couldn't poke a toe out from my duvet at night, case something came along and . . . or . . .

And then the time, erm . . . uh, the time when I was seven. And I was standing in the playground. Waiting to take my cycling proficiency test. And. And something hit me on the head. It was a shoe. A man's shoe. And it came straight down. Not across. It didn't have, like, an arc, like it had been thrown. It had fallen straight down. I picked it up. And I looked around; no one was looking, no one had seen. There was no laughing, no giggling. And on everyone's feet were two shoes. And it was a man's shoe anyway.

Jacqui Do you still have it?

Robin A black . . . a smart, black, size-eleven shoe. I looked up to see if there were any planes overhead, couldn't see any. I couldn't see a damn thing.

Pause.

Jacqui Did you pass your cycling proficiency?

Robin No. No, I turned round. Left the playground. And walked home.

It's my fault. I'm told. By the people my mum sends to insult me. I indulged in the fear, I willed it to become all-consuming, apparently. I'm the kind of character that needs something such as this to patch together an identity. So there you go.

Jacqui It has been a long time.

Robin Look who's talking.

Jacqui I'm not . . . I'm saying for me it's only been a matter of years. I mean, when was the last time you went out?

Robin Uh, it didn't go very well. I'll say that much. And, and proved how I'm not ready. Despite everyone –

Jacqui What happened? You don't have to say.

Robin It was. When my dad died. And it was his funeral. And I got to the end of the path, through the gate. Uh. Under the big tree by my road. It was pissing it down.

He enters the centre space. Under a tree. Rain and thunder. He holds himself tight.

Everyone was waiting in the cars. Mum. My brother, Mark. They, they'd tried to make it as easy as possible for me. The whole procession, pulling right up to my house. All I had to do was run across the road and get in. But then once I'm in the car, what then? Start screaming, have a panic attack? Mark and Mum had got sick of tugging on me, getting wet. Now they're just sat in the front car. Faces appearing intermittently between the sweeps of the windscreen wipers. Imploring me just to come that little bit further. But I can't. Looking at the hearse. 'Dad', written in flowers. I want to so much. So much. But I can't. My brother's face. I was ruining everything. But I'd gone as far as I could. So I turned around, and walked back inside.

He re-enters his house. Sits. Silence.

When they came back, my mum went next door to say thank you for something or other. I asked Mark how it had gone, and he said, 'Fine.' And then he hit me in the stomach. And it hurt. And I deserved it. But then as I was trying to stand he hit me again. And I didn't think I deserved that. I was the one who had missed the funeral and I'd missed it because it was becoming about me and I didn't want it to be about me, it was meant to be about Dad, and I couldn't understand why he couldn't understand that. I had wanted to go and stand up and talk about him. About the way he would do some proper old-school whistling as he mowed the lawn and the way he would drum with a fork on the biscuit tin; I'd wanted to do that. Mark went on about funerals being for the living, not the dead. And that day had been for Mum. And I had let her down. We haven't really spoken since; not properly. And I don't think that's fair.

Pause.

Jacqui Is your mum OK, now? Is she . . . seeing anyone else, or –

Robin No. She'd never do that. She's one of those. In it till the very end, type thing.

Jacqui Almost unheard of now.

Robin I'll always be grateful that . . . for my – that my mum and dad . . . you know. I couldn't have handled that. With everything else, what with all the other things I felt I had to deal with; that would have pushed me over the edge, I reckon. A broken home.

Jacqui Don't say that, 'broken'. Hate that.

Robin Sorry.

Jacqui Broken implies something that needs fixing. They often work. Very well.

Robin Of course. (*Beat.*) Even a broken home is right twice a day. Ey?

Jacqui That's a watch.

Robin Yes I know that.

Jacqui Oh right. Yes. Very good.

Evening. **Jacqui***'s room.* **Jacqui** *on her bed.* **Reece** *sitting. They drink hot chocolate.* **Reece** *is in overalls – he's just back from work.*

Reece Takes you back, ey?

Jacqui It's lovely. Thank you.

Reece 'Member when I'd sneak it up to your room? Yours and David's. Behind Mum's back. Huh. She'd always be going on about your bloody teeth. 'That hot chocolate. Ruddy well eats their teeth.' Well, it ruddy hasn't, has it? Look at you, early twenties, perfect teeth. Let's see 'em.

Jacqui *smiles a toothy grin.*

Reece Yeah, see, perfect smile.

Jacqui How's everything going with Julie?

Reece Oh fine, you know. We're just friends.

Jacqui It's all right, Dad.

Reece We are, we're just friends. Can't a fella be friends with a woman and they just be friends?

Jacqui You should invite her round more.

Reece (*shrugs*) I dunno.

Jacqui Why don't you invite her round tonight?

Reece Nah, she's at pilates or yogalates or whichever one it is, Wednesdays. Thing I don't understand is, they all go out on the piss after, and sometimes a bag of bloody chips. One cancels out the other, she says. It's like 'offsetting'. Leaves me thinking, well why are you spending all that money to end up staying exactly the bloody same? Don't ask me, Jacqui love, I don't ask myself.

Sips his drink.

Christmas, this always reminds me of. Christmas Eve. What were them Plasticine things we used to watch? 'Round Christmas time. That dog, with the –

Jacqui Oh, Wallace and Gromit.

Reece Wallace and Gromit! Ha ha. Yeah. That dog.

(Yeah, Wallace and Gromit.)

Sips his drink.

Jacqui How was work today?

Reece Urgh. All right. Not one bugger answered.

Jacqui Not one?

Reece Not bloody one; can you . . . ? I read two meters that were outside, but the rest . . . Charlie'll think I took the day off when I see him tomorrow. Not my fault though, is it?

Sips his drink.

You?

Jacqui Yeah. 'S OK.

Reece Quiet at moment, is it? What with everything, is it?

Jacqui Don't really know. I get sent my work and I do it and I send it back. You know.

Reece Lot of jobs going though, aren't there? Jobs being lost. Your thingy, your sector.

Jacqui I don't really know, Dad.

Reece I guess you might be more vulnerable, ey? If they're looking for cutbacks, people to go, I mean. Well. What with you not around. With you being 'remote', as it were . . .

Jacqui No one's said anything, Dad.

Reece Right. Good. That's good.

Jacqui Are you all right?

Reece I'm fine. What, me? Oh yeah, no I'm fine, love. Always fine. You?

Jacqui Yeah, you know.

Reece Not really, Jacqui. I don't always really know, you know. It – I can't . . .

I love having you here, you know that.

Jacqui Dad –

Reece It's lovely having you back. With David in America and everything. I can't believe it sometimes, me. My two kids, how well you've done, from these – what do they say? These 'humble origins'. Huh. You in London. Well, before the . . . and David. Over in 'America'. Huh. I can't believe it sometimes. Very proud, you know.

Jacqui . . . Thank you.

Reece You've done so well. And I'd hate to see it go to waste, you know.

Jacqui Dad –

Reece It's not that I don't like having you back, because I do. It's just. You're better than this place, Jacqui. You're better than me.

Jacqui Come on –

Reece You should be out there, love. Living. Doing.

Jacqui I just need this time. To get better.

Reece And there's no, like, medicine, or –

Jacqui It's not that kind of illness, Dad.

Reece Oh, I know, love. I know that, God only knows. 'Head' stuff. Saw it in my mam. No rhyme or reason to the things that go on up there sometimes, love, I know that.

I just hate to see you not happy, Jacqui. And I think it's time we started working on that. I've no idea how, but I think it's time we starting looking at making you happy.

First thing to prescribe is hot chocolate. There, that's done. Check. That's that one off the list. Right. So. What's next?

Jacqui (*smiles*) A cuddle?

Reece Right. Right-oh. OK. Let me see if we've got any in stock, just a minute,

(*Moves close to her.*) Ah. Here we are.

Reece *hugs* **Jacqui**. *Then harder. Pause . . .*

Reece Come on, now, don't want to OD, do you?

Jacqui I don't think I could ever OD on this.

Robin *in his house.* **Jacqui** *in her room.* **Jacqui** *is holding a letter.*

Robin Hey.

Jacqui Hey. (*Gesturing the letter.*) Your handwriting.

Robin Yep.

Jacqui What is it?

Robin Why do people always say that? Just open it.

Jacqui *starts opening.*

Robin You've not been online as much. Past few days.

Jacqui (*stops opening; pause*) I know. Just. I'm trying to sort a couple of things out.

Robin Work things?

Jacqui No. No. Thing things.

Robin Thing things?

Jacqui Life things. Me things. Head – you know, head things.

Pause.

Robin It's a birthday present.

Jacqui Oh. (*Goes back to opening.*) Erm. Early.

Robin I know. Not for a fortnight. But you need it before. To practice.

Jacqui (*opens; reads*) Oh. Huh. Jive lessons?

Robin Yup.

Jacqui (*laughs*) Uh . . .

Robin Ages ago, you said you wanted to learn jive after seeing it on, on *Strictly Come Dancing*. I said we should learn together.

Jacqui Erm. God. OK. Th-thank you. Erm. Well. Obvious question.

Robin They can come to your house. It's a 'him', he can . . . can come and give us each lessons, and then we can . . . you know, together, just pretend. Thought it would be fun.

Jacqui Oh God, of course. Yes, no, I . . . thank you. Of course.

It . . . it's still just pretend, though. Isn't it? It can never beat the real thing. You know that, don't you?

Robin Ye-es. (*Beat.*) Is anything the matter?

Jacqui I guess I want to know. What we're doing. Where . . . where we are.

Robin 'Where we are.' I think we might have just wandered into an episode of *Dawson's Creek*. (*American accent.*) 'Where we are.'

Jacqui Thank you, that's funny.

Robin We're making it bearable for each other. Aren't we?

Jacqui Erm. I need more than that. I don't want it to be bearable. I want it to be cured.

Robin I want it to be cured.

Jacqui Do you?

Robin What kind of – ?

Jacqui I want to dance with you for real one day, Robin. Actually *be* in the same . . .

Robin Y– We . . . I . . . I . . .

Jacqui Don't be mad at me.

Robin Why? What, why?

Jacqui I contacted that guy.

Robin What guy? / John?

Jacqui John.

Robin Why?

Jacqui Because I want to get fixed, Robin. I want to leave here. I can't do this for ever. Why do you want to stay like this, / this isn't life.

Robin The hell has / he been saying?!

Jacqui Stop reading about it and bloody do it.

Robin This isn't you, / this is him, this is.

Jacqui 'Robin Mays. Who learnt his life from a book!' That's no, that's no / way to –

Robin Oh Jesus!

Jacqui I don't think. (*Pause. Calmer.*) I don't think there's any point in us pursuing anything if it's going to stay like this. It's not enough, Robin. It's not enough.

Robin Well. Hey, well . . . (*Pause.*) If, if, if (shh). If you get, if you get . . . (come on). If *you* get fixed, you could come round here. You could . . . maybe even . . . / stay –

Jacqui Don't you want to leave your, your, your *cell*?

Robin Oh God, here we go, 'my sanctuary / is my cell'.

Jacqui So what? You expect me to overcome *my* fear, but not you yours? Come on!

Robin What, you want me to leave? Come round to yours?

Jacqui I . . . (*Sighs.*) I can't afford to feel things for someone . . . who isn't around. I haven't got enough left in me to do that.

Robin (*grabbing his coat, making to leave*) Fine, I'll have a panic attack, cry like a baby in the street, that what you want? / Have a fit outside my house?

Jacqui I want to have something that isn't pretend!

Robin Knock my confidence, set me / back another year.

Jacqui I want to have something that isn't pretend!

Robin *paces up and down towards the door. He opens it and takes a step out.*

Jacqui Robin, for God's sake!

Robin *turns and collapses back on to the floor. He curls up, holding his head. Pause.*

Jacqui Robin . . .

Robin . . . I can't. Please. I can't . . .

Jacqui OK. OK . . .

But I have to try.

And I probably can't do that with you. You make it too easy to stay like this.

I have to try . . .

Robin (*stands; beat; nods*) You should, um. Keep the dance lessons.

Jacqui No, I . . . You can – They must have been expensive. You can probably get your –

Robin Please, just take them. Do them. Learn. I, I . . . might do too. Still. As well. Who knows.

Jacqui . . . Thank you.

Robin *alone in his house. He opens a drawer in his desk, and takes out the black shoe that fell from the sky. He holds it against his head, and sits on the floor.*

Jacqui *alone in her room. She opens a music box. And winds it up. She places it down and it plays. A model princess turning inside . . .*

Reece *stands with* **Lesley** *at his doorway.*

Lesley I just thought it was worth a try again. You know.

Reece Oh yes. Yes, no, always worth a try. I'm sorry she hasn't come down.

Lesley That's OK. I'll try again tomorrow, if that's all right.

Reece Well, you can if you like. Although I rather feel you might be wasting your time. It isn't me, you understand, it doesn't bother me –

Lesley Right.

Reece It's just I rather get the impression she doesn't want to have contact with . . . you know, with your lad at the moment, and thus . . . you know, vis-à-vis, vice versa –

Lesley Right.

Reece I think she thinks it wouldn't help. With the 'process', you see. That chap seems to be doing a lot of good.

Lesley John?

Reece Yes. Had her standing right here this morning. Just on the other side of the door.

Lesley What? Outside?

Reece Yup. One hand firmly on the handle, mind, huhuh. But nevertheless, feet outside.

Lesley Really? So . . . so soon? Well, that's . . . (*Beat.*) She must. Really want to get better. Then. That's . . . that's really good.

Pause. She goes to leave. Stops.

Always think we know best, though, don't we? You spend so long trying to get rid of them, but deep down, deep deep down, the thought of them not needing you, the thought of you being, like, 'redundant', makes me feel sick sometimes. Makes me go all dizzy and I need a sit down. Huh.

Reece Like I say, I did try to get her to see you. But it's complicated. You know.

Lesley Yes, of . . . These things often are.

Reece Exactly.

Lesley I think that things are more complicated than they ever used to be.

Reece You're right. You are right there.

Lesley I look around sometimes. Sometimes I just stop and look and I think to myself. I'm sure this didn't used to be . . . quite so complicated.

Pause.

Tell her well done. From me. That's . . . that really is very, very good.

Darkness. **John** *and* **Robin** *speaking over the phone.*

John (*off*) Jacqui has realised, has had the revelation, the one you refuse to have, that the thing stopping her going outside was in fact something else.

Robin (*off*) Stop trying to take her away from me.

John (*off*) That it isn't real, Robin. This fear of yours. It's a device. It's an excuse.

Robin (*off*) Mir Space Station, April 2005, falls into the / South Pacific, close to Fiji.

John (*off*) Robin. Robin, come on.

Robin (*off*) BeppoSAX. Dutch Italian Satellite, dropped out of orbit before scheduled.

John (*off*) Robin, I know / you have a whole bag of facts ready to counter my –

Robin (*off*) Lands luckily into a deserted area of the Pacific Ocean, but the threat was real enough to put thirty-nine separate countries / on high alert –

John (*off*) Until you ask yourself what it is you're actually afraid of. What besides things dropping from the sky, things that you know, deep down, if you ever had the courage to look, that you know Aren't Ever Going To Fall.

Robin (*off*) What goes up, John. What goes up. / Must come down.

John (*off*) Can sometimes stay up, Robin.

Robin (*off*) Stop my mum from trying to help. I don't want her to help me.

John (*off*) Your / mother is –

Robin (*off*) January 1997. Woman, Oklahoma, hit on the head by orbital / debris from –

John (*off*) If you confront what you're *actually* afraid of, Robin, then we could diagnose it. And then cure it. If only you wanted to get better.

Robin (*off*) People keep saying that. Like it's a disease. I'm the most contented person I know. It's you who has the problems. I look at people from my window, see you on the television, listen on the radio. Your problems sound so horrible. My life is simple.

John (*off*) Robin, you're life isn't real. You need to grow up.

Robin (*off*) Isn't the most important thing to be happy? However you find it? Just to be happy?

Jacqui*'s room.* **Jacqui** *sits on her bed.* **Lesley** *stands. Looks around.*

Lesley It's nice. Nice that your dad kept it the way . . . you know, the way it was.

Jacqui I guess.

Lesley I changed Robin's. Never really thought about that until now, guess that might have annoyed him a little bit. I just didn't think. As soon as he went off to uni, bam. I was in. Posters down. Duvet cover off. It's a guest bedroom, now. So it's still a bedroom, but . . . I say Robin's, it was Robin and Mark's, they used to share, had bunk-beds. Ooh, did they used to fight. Huh. I'd be downstairs, doing whatever, and you'd just hear this 'thud'. And I knew it'd be one throwing one of them off the other one's bed. And I'd be able to guess from the size of the thud whether whoever had fallen from the bottom or the top, and that'd tell me who it was that had been thrown. Mark was on the top, see. Robin bottom. If Robin was annoyed, and feeling brave enough, he'd push Mark's mattress up with his feet. Used to wind Mark up so much.

Does it bother you, having a single bed? I suppose you had a double in your flat in London. Or even a king size. Wouldn't bother me, you know, I don't move around at all; certainly don't move over to the other side of the bed, you'd never catch me over there. Don't know why, really, I just find myself waking up in the exact same spot I went to sleep in, you know? Guess that's what comes of sleeping in the same bed as someone else for twenty-seven years.

I hope you don't mind me coming up.

Jacqui It is a little strange.

Lesley Is it?

Jacqui I can't remember the last time anyone was in my room except my dad. (*Pause.*) Used to love having people in here. As a kid.

Lesley Yeah?

Jacqui Having the girls round for sleepovers. Michelle. Andrea. Rachel. Do girls still do that? Sleepovers?

Lesley I expect they do, yes.

Jacqui (*beat*) Darren Connolly. Huh. Remember when he came in here. After school one day. That was weird. I didn't have a clue what I was doing. I was so scared . . .

Lesley Is your dad all right, on his own, does he cope?

Jacqui He's seen some other people. Not in any kind of committed way. I don't think he can be bothered any more, actually. I wish he would.

Lesley Still have a candle for your mum a bit, does he? – that what they say? 'Hold a torch for' or something.

Jacqui I couldn't tell you.

Lesley When was it she left? Do you mind me asking?

Jacqui I do a little bit.

Lesley Oh, right.

Jacqui She left more than once. Came back. More than once.

Lesley Right.

Jacqui I think it's better to either have someone or not.

Lesley Right.

Jacqui Back when I had friends, when I had boyfriends, back when I had a life, in London when I had a life, it always struck me that the single people I knew were actually quite happy and the people in relationships I knew were happy but the people who had a crush on or yearned for or secretly loved or were kind of 'with' but kind of 'not with' someone . . . that they were the most unhappy.

So, I think it's better to either just have someone or just not.

Lesley But better to have someone than not, ey?

Pause.

How far did you get today?

Jacqui To the house across the street; I touched the wall.

Lesley You touched the wall!

Jacqui Ran out. Screaming. Touched the wall. Ran back. Shut the door.

Lesley Well that's . . . !

Jacqui And I'm taking my dance lessons. Inside, but –

Lesley Well. You . . . You Are Doing Really Well.

Jacqui I am. I am doing well. So I don't . . . I can't jeopardise –

Lesley The thing is, Robin needs something to strive for, to fight for, in order to make that leap, and he's never had anything worth fighting before and I just think –

Jacqui I don't think Robin . . . actually wants to change, Lesley. And –

Lesley Would you like me to drive you back?

Jacqui No thank you.

Lesley It's only a couple of minutes.

Jacqui No thank you.

Lesley I don't mind.

Jacqui I can't. I'm not read– and, it wouldn't help him to –

Lesley I could bring you back, after.

Jacqui No. But thank you.

Lesley That's all right. You're welcome.

In the centre space. A firework goes off. And then another. And then more.

Jacqui *leans in, watching from her room.* **Robin** *from his.*

Robin Can you see them?

Jacqui Yes! YES! They're beautiful! How did you . . . ?

Robin They're um, from a box, you just, you just, light and run. Huh.

Jacqui So you went outside? Into your garden?

Robin I. Well. I. Yeah. I. Ran outside. And then, huh, and then ran back in.

Jacqui Robin, that's . . . that's amazing. Well done.

Robin Well. It's your birthday in, (*Checks his watch.*) ooh, eleven minutes. So.

Jacqui Thank you. (*Watches.*) So that's where you live. Over there.

Robin Yeah. Yeah, this is where I live.

So. What do you think? Give it a go?

Jacqui (*pause*) I've been doing. So well, Robin –

Robin Just to see. Just so I can show you. How it could work.

Pause.

Jacqui (*smiles*) OK.

Blackout on the rooms. The fireworks continue for a while, before fizzling out . . .

Jacqui *in her room, glammed up in a dress.* **Robin** *in his house, wearing a suit. Each has half a dining table in their rooms that are split at the cut-off point – two parts of the same whole. Candles are lit.* **Robin** *already has a plate of food at his table.*

Jacqui (*twirling*) Well?

Robin You look amazing.

Knock at her bedroom. **Jimmy** *stands holding a thermos bag and a bottle of wine.*

Jacqui And who could this be? (*Answering.*) Well, hello, sir.

Jimmy Good evening, madam. I will be your waiter for this evening. May I present to you your meal?

Jacqui Why, thank you. (*Smelling.*) Hmm, lovely.

Jimmy And. (*Sprays her wrist with aftershave.*) Your date wishes you to know how he smells this evening.

Jacqui (*sniffing her wrist*) Hmm, gorgeous. Wow. Very nice.

Jimmy The gentlemen also requested that I deliver this. (*Kisses her on the cheek.*) With his best wishes.

If you need anything just call and I'm only thirty to forty minutes away.

Jacqui Thanks, Jimmy.

Jimmy You look stunning.

Jimmy *leaves.* **Jacqui** *goes to the table, removing a plate from the heat-sealed bag, removing the cling film, and sitting at the table with the wine.* **Robin** *also sits.*

Robin Shall we?

Jacqui I can't believe you cooked this, looks amazing.

Robin Is it still warm?

Jacqui I'm sure it's fine.

Robin Wine?

Jacqui Thank you. Shall I pour myself?

Robin Uh, if you wouldn't mind.

Jacqui There. (*Tasting the food.*) Mm. *Mm*. Wow. Well done you.

Robin 'S all right.

Jacqui It's better than all right, stop putting yourself down.

Robin It's nice not to just cook for one. For once. Happy birthday.

Jacqui So. How was your day at work today, darling, all right?

Robin Oh, fine. Fine. Got the first draft of my next book to the agent, you know. You?

Jacqui Oh, I decided to work from home today.

Robin Really?

Jacqui Hmm. So. When are you going to tell me about your new book?

Robin Ugh. Nah. I'll only make it sound rubbish.

Jacqui No, you won't. Come on.

Robin Really. Honestly. No. I, I don't like . . . before it's done, I –

Jacqui False modesty. What's it called?

Robin (*sighs*) It, it's called . . . no. OK. It's called . . . (*Pause. Sighs.*) *Poor Poor Pluto.* And. It's about . . . well, it's, the characters are. Um. Are the planets. In the solar system. And, (see I'm making it sound) . . . and, uh, Pluto. Is the main character. And all it is, is he gets told, by the others, that he isn't a proper planet any more.

Jacqui Awh.

Robin Exactly. So. And he's always been kind of skirting around on the peripheries of the, of the proverbial playground as it were anyway, but *now* . . . Well, officially he, it was downgraded to, erm . . . Well, and don't read too much into this, but now I've said that, of course you're going . . . uh, to a satellite. Huh. Coinc– oddly enough. Like the moon of something else. So condemned into a supporting role. Doing what satellites do. Orbiting around the main body. Watching. But never . . . getting involved. Just watching.

Jacqui Huh. Where *do* you get your ideas from? (*Smiles.*) I hope it's a success for you.

Robin Y-we-ye-well . . . (Shh.) Thank you.

Music pumps out. **Robin** *and* **Jacqui** *spin away their chairs, brush themselves down, face each other, and count themselves in. They begin a jive – despite the distance between them, they could almost be dancing together. They laugh and giggle but continue, mock-seriously. Finishing with a flourish.*

Late night. **Jacqui** *is sprawled on the bed.* **Robin** *in his room.*

Jacqui You know, if the writing thing doesn't work out, which I'm sure it will, but if it doesn't, I reckon as a chef you'd do bloody well. Or even a professional dancer.

Robin Well, I'll need a partner.

Jacqui You went to a lot of trouble.

Robin Not really.

Jacqui No you did. (*Beat. As mock-American girl.*) 'This was my bestest birthday ever!'

Robin Hmm.

Jacqui *smells her wrist. Smiles. Smells it again.*

Jacqui Well I'd invite you in for coffee, but . . .

Robin *gasps playfully.*

Jacqui But I'm not that kind of girl.

Robin And I'm not that kind of boy.

Jacqui Good. So. (*Standing.*) I guess . . . (*Wobbling on her feet.*) Whoop.

Robin You all right?

Jacqui Yep. Yep. These heels. It's been a while.

Robin Oh, it's the heels.

Jacqui Yes. It is. So. (*Sighs.*) So. I guess this is where we leave it.

Robin *smiles weakly, and nods. Long, heavy pause.*

Jacqui Thank you, Robin, for a . . . for a really nice birthday.

Robin Hmm . . .

It isn't enough, is it?

Pause.

Jacqui It's been a lovely / evening.

Robin It isn't enough. Where from here, what next? Tomorrow? It isn't enough. (*Pause.*) I . . . I don't want to lose this.

Jacqui We don't have to lose this. I just don't think it can . . . I don't think it can be anything *more* than this. If it *is* this. Do you see? I'm sorry.

Robin Then . . . then . . . then let's . . . let's do it.

Jacqui Do what?

Robin Let, let's, let's . . . let, let's, let's meet. I'll, I'll . . . I'll meet you.

Jacqui What do you mean?

Robin Let's do this. Let, let's meet. I'll, I can, I'll l-l-leave. I'll come to you. And you to me. And, and we'll, we'll. Meet.

Pause.

Jacqui You'll . . . ?

Robin Let's meet. Let's just do it. Let's just try, I'm . . . I'm willing to . . . (shit!) I'll try. Now. Soon, now.

Jacqui (*beat; laughs*) Seriously? What? No. Seriously?

Robin Yes?

Jacqui All right, then. (*Beat; laughs.*) Oh my God!

Robin (*laughs; cries a bit; laughs*) Shit.

Jacqui How? When? Oh my God, no. Really? No!

Robin Let's – we need – let's . . . I don't know, find somewhere. Halfway between. But it, it has to be soon, otherwise, I'll . . . shit. Jesus! Has to be soon. Has to be –

Jacqui Tomorrow?

Robin OK.

Pause. **Jacqui** *squeals, excited and terrified.*

Robin (*laughs, drops to his knees, stands again*) Oh God, oh God, oh shit, uh –

Jacqui But, but *you*, you haven't been out in –

Robin Well, I, I, I, I . . . I could, I could do with the, the, huh, the Fresh Air. Uh . . .

Jacqui No. No, we're going to wake up tomorrow and not do it. I know it.

Robin No.

Jacqui It's because we've been drinking.

Robin No, no. I will. I want to. I can. I will. We just need to plan it.

> **Robin** (*speaking out, getting changed as he does*) I don't believe a word I'm saying. Just so you know. I'm just a bystander, watching the words come out my mouth, and thinking, 'Christ, you're on your own there, mate. Enjoy.' And I'm just humouring him. But things get away from you, and once you're in the thing, the carriage, and the bar comes down over your lap and you're setting off up the roller coaster there isn't much you can do, is there? Except scream your tits off, of course.

Jacqui *in her room, changed to go out.* **Robin** *the same in his. He taps on his computer. On the screen at the back, a street map of the local area.*

Jacqui You OK?

Robin No. You?

Jacqui No, not even a little bit.

Robin Good. At least we're on the same page. Huh.

Jacqui Oh my God . . .

Robin I've got your mobile number, if there's a problem, I'll find, find a phone box. Do they still exist? Round here? Phone boxes?

Jacqui Uh, yeah, s'pose. Shit.

Robin So. One o'clock. Under the bridge. (*Pointing at the map.*) By the side of the park

Jacqui One o'clock. Under the bridge. One o'clock. That's half an hour. That's fine. Ha. Under the bridge. Strong, sturdy bridge.

Smiles nervously. Stops. Deep breath.

I w-wish you had a, a mobile.

Robin Nev– never needed one. (*Attempting a jokey tone, but failing.*) Plus they, they attract satellites, so . . . (*Pause.*)

Jacqui How do I look?

Robin Fine. Is it warm outside? This too much?

Jacqui Dunno. You got everything?

Robin I don't . . . know what I need. Oh God.

Goes to be sick. Gags a bit. Gathers himself.

I'm. Sorry, if . . . if I don't make it –

Jacqui Don't. You will. Don't say that. It's just this first part that's the worst. Once we're out. Once we're . . . maybe we should have done taxis.

Robin No! No, we – if we did that, then what? Get the taxis to take us back to one of ours and then what? Get them to wait, and take one of us back, and then . . . no, if we're doing it, then . . . then we're bloody –

Jacqui No, you're right. (You're right.) Huh. Just think in, in about five minutes' time we'll be as close to each other as we are to home.

Robin Yeah. Yeah. A bit like what the Russian army used to do.

Jacqui Is it?

Robin Yeah.

Jacqui Oh. That's good then.

Robin Whenever they were invaded, from the east, they, they, the Russians, they'd retreat back. Back and back into their own country, sort of scorching the land as they, they went, so the enemy couldn't get any food or shelter. And eventually they'd been lured so far in, the enemy were just too far from home to go back, but going forward there was just more, uh, more barren land, and so they were just kinda stuck.

Jacqui Oh. What happened, then?

Robin Well. They all, they all died. So.

Jacqui Oh. OK. 'S a good story.

Robin Thank you.

Jacqui My answer machine! Need to record a message, for the first time in . . . (*Presses button on answer machine. It beeps.*) Uh, hello, you've reached Jacqui's phone. Um . . . ha-hard as it may be to believe, I'm actually out. So. So leave a message. Or call my mobile, erm. If, if you don't have my mobile number then, uh . . . well, then, there's a reason for that, thanks, bye. (*Presses the button.*) So-o-o . . .

Robin So. (*Sighs heavily.*) I do, I really do, erm . . . I really do think that, that I . . . Jacqui, I really do believe that in the past months I've started to fa– that I am in, in . . . or I least could be one day, in, in lo–

Jacqui Wait. Wait. Save it. For face to face.

Robin Face to face. (*Nods.*) Huh. Face to face. Just the thought of being able to . . . to touch you. Not, no, not in, in that –

Robin I didn't mean –

Robin I mean . . . just . . . for you to just be real. For you to just be real.

Jacqui I'm going to turn you off now.

Robin No, wait, don't, why?!

Jacqui I don't want you to see me leave.

Robin What, no, I need to see you go otherwise –

Jacqui I need to . . . (*Sighs.*) 'put' something else on, but I don't want you to see it –

Robin Don't be silly, I –

Jacqui Fine! Just . . .

She retrieves a London beefeater's hat and puts it on.

Jacqui But don't ask me why, it just makes me feel better. Protected. Better.

Robin I wish I had something. Oh.

He grabs an umbrella and shows her. They smile.

(*Deep breath.*) So.

Jacqui So. You could write about this one day. Our own little adventure story.

Jacqui One to tell you all. When we get back.

Robin Yeah. If it ends well.

Jacqui Course it will end well. How would it end?

Robin I dunno. How will it end?

Jacqui With a, a happy ending. I hope. In colour.

Robin Yeah. Course. Happy ending would be good.

Jacqui Under the bridge, one o'clock.

Robin Under the bridge. One o'clock. (*Deep breath.*) Later skater.

Jacqui (*smiles*) In a bit, shit.

Robin *goes to his door.* **Jacqui** *to hers. They open them.* **Jacqui** *rests her head against the frame.* **Robin** *weakens and drops to his knees, but quickly struggles back up. Beat. They both bolt out, screaming,* **Robin** *opening the umbrella as he goes . . .*

Dim lights up on **Jacqui***'s room. The phone rings. After a few seconds it goes to voicemail, and we hear the first moments of her recorded message.*

Lights down.

Dim lights up on **Jacqui***'s room as she enters. She turns the light on.*

She stands motionless for a while. She takes her shoes off. Tosses them down.

She looks over at **Robin***'s room, in semi-darkness still . . .*

She notices the red light flashing on her machine. She presses play. It beeps.

Answering machine You have . . . one . . . message.

Lights down.

Robin*'s house.* **Robin** *is sitting on the floor.* **Lesley** *sits nearby. Silence.*

Lesley Did you have that casserole in the end? All right, was it?

Pause. **Robin** *nods.*

Lesley So you tried the path thing, then, did you? That's what this is about?

Well, that's wonderful, that is. Well done, love. How far did you get?

Robin End of the path.

Lesley Right to the end?

Robin And a bit further.

Lesley And a bit further?! To where?

Robin Past the tree.

Lesley Past the *tree*?! Well that's wonderful, that is. Well done.

Robin It wasn't wonderful.

Lesley Now don't you put yourself down, Robin, don't you put yourself down, that's marvellous, that's more than marvellous, that's flippin' miraculous, that, well done.

Robin I was meant to go further.

Lesley What happened?

Robin I was meant to go all the way to her.

Under the bridge.

Screaming, off. Getting closer.

Jacqui *arrives at speed, wearing her beefeater hat. She hits the floor. She stands, still screaming, but now happy, giddy, jumping up and down, clapping and squealing.*

Jacqui Argh – I – did – it, I bloody did it! I . . . I . . . argh!

She slowly gathers herself, and looks around for any sign of **Robin**. *The distant sound of a phone ringing. The opening of* **Jacqui**'*s voicemail . . . as lights rise nearby on:*

A phone box. **Robin** *leaning against the side, catching his breath. Phone to his ear.*

Even though he is clearly far apart from **Jacqui**, *here they appear quite close.* **Robin** *is watching her. The message on* **Jacqui**'*s answer machine ends, followed by the beep.*

Robin (*speaking into the phone*) Jacqui. (Jacqui.)

He leans out with the receiver, watching her. He rests his head against the side.

(*Sighs.*) I'm, erm . . . I'm in a phone box. And I can see you. You're waiting for me.

I'm, um . . . uh . . . I'm, I'm so sorry. (*Sighs. Groans.*) I'm so sorry.

Uh, you see. What's happened is. (What's happened is.)

The line beeps He inserts coins.

Erm. Ha. I got here! I got here, isn't that – I didn't think I would and I nearly didn't but I did and it was hell, it was hell on earth, but I did, and I just kept running and I got here and . . . and I was afraid. I was really – but I . . . for as long as I can remember, I've been afraid. Uh, which isn't good. Huh. Erm. It isn't good to be, to be this afraid. Of things. I don't think. But, but being brave, as I understand it, being brave . . . it, it doesn't mean not being afraid, it means doing it, doing it in spite of being . . . I'm rambling, now, the point is. Jacqui. Huh.

The point. Is.

That I've been so focused on, on . . . on things falling from the sky and, and beating that . . . (*Pause.*) I'm sorry. What am I saying? I'm saying. That there's something more frightening now than, than falling satellites.

The line beeps. He inserts coins.

It's been such a long time. Since anyone. Um. Cared about me, uh, in that way. If, if ever. And I, uh . . . I suppose I'm a little bit concerned about that now. Actually. Huh. That 'responsibility'. Um. Of, of being . . . Worth It. And seeing you here. Standing only, only yards away. Well. You're real. And. Erm. And I'm not sure I can handle that. I'm a, a . . . huh . . . I'm a bystander, Jacqui. It, that's all I know. (That's all I know.)

He leans his head against the side. Hits his head against the side. Comes back up.

You. Wouldn't, uh . . . you wouldn't like me. In real life. Very much, I'm . . . I'm not one of those kinds of people that people really like. And I don't want to, to, lose . . . the thing we had. But, you know like all good things . . . well, you know, what, what goes up. Ey? (What goes up.)

He makes to replace the receiver, but stops, looking at **Jacqui** *again.*

Robin You, you really do look . . . really very good, though. You know. In the face.

So good I, I can hardly breathe, actually.

The line beeps. He makes to replace the receiver, but has a quick beat.

Oh and, uh, I love you.

He replaces the receiver. He watches **Jacqui***. He looks up at the sky, and exits at speed.* **Jacqui** *stands waiting under the arch. The lights fade out on her. Blackout.*

Robin*'s room.* **Robin** *on the floor.* **Lesley** *seated.*

Lesley You know, me and your dad could never find one another. We'd always be like magnets that repulsed – repel? Repelled each other. I remember one time I lost him in ASDA.

He'd always go wandering off, and so I call him on his mobile and we're trying to work out where the other one is and it only turns out we're standing bloody next to each other. Right there, by the fish fingers. So it just goes to show.

Pause.

What's that in you hand?

Robin A letter.

Lesley For her? You gonna post it?

Robin I've got a courier coming round.

Lesley Tell her yourself. I could drive you round.

Robin It's cheating. And I wouldn't . . . I wouldn't know what to do when I got there.

Lesley It's the same for everyone. A step into the unknown. Reminds me of / when –

Robin I know what's . . .

Lesley Oh, sorry, go on.

Robin I know what's ahead of me, scorched earth.

Lesley Scorched earth?

Robin Like what the Russians did.

Lesley Like what the Russians did?

Robin Mum, you're doing it again.

Lesley What did the Russians do, though, love? Sorry.

Robin To the advancing enemy – burn the land. So that when they're so far in, they're trapped. All that's behind them is scorched land. All that's ahead of them is scorched land. All that's around them is scorched frigging land . . .

Lesley And what did they do?

Robin (*shrugs*) Carried on.

Silence. **Lesley** *clearly thinking about this . . .*

Lesley Well. You would do. Wouldn't you?

Robin (*pause*) What?

Lesley You would carry on. Wouldn't you? Because you, you know what's behind you, don't you? Nothing. Because you've seen it. And you know what's around you now, nothing again, because you can see it. And even if you are pretty sure the exact same thing is ahead of you, well . . . no point in going back or staying still, is there? At least in front there's the slightest bit of. Hope.

Beat. **Robin** *looks up at his mum . . .*

Jacqui *in her room. Later. She's facing* **Robin***'s house, which is now in darkness.*

Jacqui Hello? (*Pause.*) Robin? (*Pause.*) I got your message. (*Pause.*) Are you there? (*Pause.*) I do. Understand. You know. It hurts, and I'm disappointed, and I'm lying, I'm more than that, I'm . . . but I can't not see you again. Even though I can't forgive you, I can't lose whatever small part of you I had. So please if you're . . . How can you say I wouldn't like you very much? I . . . ? (*Struggling.*) You've broken my heart . . .

A knock on the door. **Jimmy** *calls out, off.*

Jimmy (*off*) Courier.

Jacqui Is this from you? Whatever it is, it won't be enough.

Jacqui *answers the door.* **Jimmy** *is there, dressed in out-of-work clothes.*

Jimmy Hey Jacqui.

Jacqui You're working late.

Jimmy I'm not actually meant to be working. But I thought I'd make this one last drop.

Jimmy *leads* **Robin** *in. Wearing a helmet. Silence.* **Jacqui** *stares.* **Robin** *is trembling.*

Jimmy Sign for it?

Beat. Bewildered, **Jacqui** *signs her name.* **Jimmy** *smiles, and exits, closing the door. They stare at each other. Both are shaking. Silence.* **Jacqui** *tries for normality.*

Jacqui I, I . . . just left you a, a message.

Robin Y– yeah? What . . . saying what?

Jacqui That you. Broke my heart. Huh.

Robin Oh. OK.

Jacqui I didn't mean it.

Robin (*shrugs*) Even a broken heart is right twice a day.

Jacqui . . .

Robin (*looks around*) This is . . . st-strange, being . . . 's like walking on to the set of a, of a film. You've seen. Lots of times.

Jacqui Huh.

Robin Smaller.

Jacqui It is small.

Robin No, but I mean, it *feels* . . . from watching . . . through the, um . . .

Jacqui (*tries to smile, but struggling; beat*) How was the, the, journey – ?

Robin I screamed all the way.

Jacqui Right. Yes.

Robin No, but I mean, he's a good driver, Jimmy.

Jacqui Good.

Robin Has a little, uh . . . sat-nav thing. On his bike.

Jacqui Huh.

Robin Brings people together, now. Apparently. 'Stead of keeping them apart.

Long pause.

I am going to make . . . So Many Mistakes. In this. But if you're OK with that. Then that's OK . . .

Jacqui (*pause*) Would you like a cup of tea? Or something?

Robin A cup of tea would be amazing. Thank you.

Jacqui This is very strange.

Robin It is strange.

Jacqui It's like having a stranger in my room. Like Darren Connolly.

Robin Darren Connolly?

Jacqui The last boy I had up here. Only it's not like that.

Robin Right.

Jacqui Because you're like a person I know.

Robin Right.

Jacqui Like the person I know most about in the world who knows most about me but who I've never met.

Robin Well. Let's meet.

He holds out his hand.

Hi. I'm Robin.

Jacqui (*beat; holds out her hand*) Jacqui.

They hold each other's hand – and look down at them. Slightly overcome by the touch.

Jacqui It's 'U' and 'I'. At the end.

Robin I'm so glad.

Lights down.

Methuen Drama Student Editions

Jean Anouilh *Antigone* • John Arden *Serjeant Musgrave's Dance* Alan Ayckbourn *Confusions* • Aphra Behn *The Rover* Edward Bond *Lear* • Bertolt Brecht *The Caucasian Chalk Circle* *Life of Galileo* • *Mother Courage and her Children* *The Resistible Rise of Arturo Ui* • *The Threepenny Opera* Anton Chekhov *The Cherry Orchard* • *The Seagull* • *Three Sisters* *Uncle Vanya* • Caryl Churchill *Serious Money* • *Top Girls* Shelagh Delaney *A Taste of Honey* • Euripides *Elektra* • *Medea* Dario Fo *Accidental Death of an Anarchist* • Michael Frayn *Copenhagen* John Galsworthy *Strife* • Nikolai Gogol *The Government Inspector* Robert Holman *Across Oka* • Henrik Ibsen *A Doll's House* • *Ghosts* *Hedda Gabler* • Charlotte Keatley *My Mother Said I Never Should* Bernard Kops *Dreams of Anne Frank* • Federico García Lorca *Blood Wedding* • *Doña Rosita the Spinster* (bilingual edition) • *The House of Bernarda Alba* • (bilingual edition) • *Yerma* (bilingual edition) • David Mamet *Glengarry Glen Ross* • *Oleanna* • Patrick Marber *Closer* • John Marston *The Malcontent* • Joe Orton *Loot* • Luigi Pirandello *Six Characters in Search of an Author* • Mark Ravenhill *Shopping and F***ing* • Willy Russell *Blood Brothers* • *Educating Rita* • Sophocles *Antigone* • *Oedipus the King* • Wole Soyinka *Death and the King's Horseman* • August Strindberg *Miss Julie* • J. M. Synge *The Playboy of the Western World* • Theatre Workshop *Oh What a Lovely War* Timberlake Wertenbaker *Our Country's Good* • Arnold Wesker *The Merchant* • Oscar Wilde *The Importance of Being Earnest* • Tennessee Williams *A Streetcar Named Desire* • *The Glass Menagerie*

Methuen Drama Modern Plays

include work by

Edward Albee
Jean Anouilh
John Arden
Margaretta D'Arcy
Peter Barnes
Sebastian Barry
Brendan Behan
Dermot Bolger
Edward Bond
Bertolt Brecht
Howard Brenton
Anthony Burgess
Simon Burke
Jim Cartwright
Caryl Churchill
Noël Coward
Lucinda Coxon
Sarah Daniels
Nick Darke
Nick Dear
Shelagh Delaney
David Edgar
David Eldridge
Dario Fo
Michael Frayn
John Godber
Paul Godfrey
David Greig
John Guare
Peter Handke
David Harrower
Jonathan Harvey
Iain Heggie
Declan Hughes
Terry Johnson
Sarah Kane
Charlotte Keatley
Barrie Keeffe
Howard Korder
Robert Lepage
Doug Lucie
Martin McDonagh
John McGrath
Terrence McNally
David Mamet
Patrick Marber
Arthur Miller
Mtwa, Ngema & Simon
Tom Murphy
Phyllis Nagy
Peter Nichols
Sean O'Brien
Joseph O'Connor
Joe Orton
Louise Page
Joe Penhall
Luigi Pirandello
Stephen Poliakoff
Franca Rame
Mark Ravenhill
Philip Ridley
Reginald Rose
Willy Russell
Jean-Paul Sartre
Sam Shepard
Wole Soyinka
Simon Stephens
Shelagh Stephenson
Peter Straughan
C. P. Taylor
Theatre de Complicite
Theatre Workshop
Sue Townsend
Judy Upton
Timberlake Wertenbaker
Roy Williams
Snoo Wilson
Victoria Wood

Methuen Drama Contemporary Dramatists
include

John Arden (two volumes)
Arden & D'Arcy
Peter Barnes (three volumes)
Sebastian Barry
Dermot Bolger
Edward Bond (eight volumes)
Howard Brenton
 (two volumes)
Richard Cameron
Jim Cartwright
Caryl Churchill
 (two volumes)
Sarah Daniels (two volumes)
Nick Darke
David Edgar (three volumes)
David Eldridge
Ben Elton
Dario Fo (two volumes)
Michael Frayn (three volumes)
John Godber (three volumes)
Paul Godfrey
David Greig
John Guare
Lee Hall (two volumes)
Peter Handke
Jonathan Harvey
 (two volumes)
Declan Hughes
Terry Johnson (three volumes)
Sarah Kane
Barrie Keeffe
Bernard-Marie Koltès
 (two volumes)
David Lan
Bryony Lavery
Deborah Levy
Doug Lucie
David Mamet (four volumes)
Martin McDonagh
Duncan McLean
Anthony Minghella
 (two volumes)
Tom Murphy (five volumes)
Phyllis Nagy
Anthony Neilson
Philip Osment
Gary Owen
Louise Page
Stewart Parker (two volumes)
Joe Penhall
Stephen Poliakoff
 (three volumes)
David Rabe
Mark Ravenhill
Christina Reid
Philip Ridley
Willy Russell
Eric-Emmanuel Schmitt
Ntozake Shange
Sam Shepard (two volumes)
Wole Soyinka (two volumes)
Simon Stephens
Shelagh Stephenson
David Storey (three volumes)
Sue Townsend
Judy Upton
Michel Vinaver
 (two volumes)
Arnold Wesker (two volumes)
Michael Wilcox
Roy Williams (two volumes)
Snoo Wilson (two volumes)
David Wood (two volumes)
Victoria Wood